Layer by layer, torn borders and strips add just the right texture and dimension to pages.

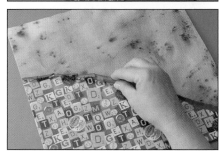

Basic Instructions

You'll Love a Deckle Ruler

What's a Deckle ruler? It's a metal ruler with a wavy edge that makes tearing borders and strips really easy and even faster than cutting.

Place your cardstock or paper on a flat surface. Position a ruler about $1/2$" to 1" from the edge of the paper (just enough so your fingers can grasp the paper firmly). Using a forceful motion, tear your paper against the edge of the ruler.

TIP: Place decorative paper face up to create a wider white edge when you tear - face down for no white edge.

TIP: For heavier paper, dampen the edge slightly with a sponge and water or use a water pen. The paper will tear more easily and more textured fibers will show along the edge.

Get a smoother line with texture by using the smooth side of the ruler.

How to Tear a Deckle Shape

To begin, draw a circle or shape on your cardstock or paper. Draw lines from the center of the shape to the edge, sort of like cutting a pie.

Poke your scissors through the center. Cut wedges to the edge of the circle, like cutting a pie.

Place a deckle ruler along the line surrounding the circle or shape. Tear the wedges out as you move the ruler around the shape.

How to Use a Clear Ruler

A clear Quilter's ruler with inch marks makes measuring easy. You can tear a straight edge quickly.

Simply place straight edge of ruler where you want to tear. You can see through the ruler and position the marks to accurately measure and tear at the same time.

Create borders and strips.

Add Interest to Torn Edges

Add another dimension to torn edges by curling the paper around an old pencil or with your fingers.

Enhance the edge with chalk ink or scrapbooker's chalks.

Age Papers with Walnut Ink

Walnut Ink is used to alter the color of a paper when it is too bright. Walnut ink is a crystal powder similar to freeze dried coffee. Mix it with water, add more crystals for a darker tint, or dilute it to make a lighter tint.

Apply Walnut ink with a paint brush, spray bottle, sponge, or drip it on. Note: Walnut ink is not acid free.

P9-APV-009

Basic Supplies

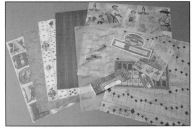

Collage Paper & Ephemera

Collaged memorabilia extends the theme and gives your page a sense of unity.

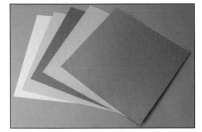

Cardstock

Textured cardstock can create the feeling of nostalgic linens or add a bold graphic to a masculine page.

Mounts

Need a ready-to-go frame? These mounts are great!

Transparency Sheets

Add color, text and images in a new texture.

Basic Adhesives

Create dimension with Zots, Mounting squares and other products.

At Home and Abroad

Keep your journal notes for scrapbooking and other hobbies in a book that is fun to use. Collage the cover of an ordinary notebook and make it your own.

Friends Journal
by Delores Frantz

MATERIALS: *Design Originals:* Collage paper (#0600 Dominoes); Printed Mounts (#0986 Color Games); Transparency sheets (#0622 Beauties) • Red handmade paper • White cardstock • 7½" x 9¾" Journal • *ColorBox* Cat's Eye Chestnut Roan ink • 6" *DMC* Red cotton crochet thread • 36" *Offray* ⅝" sheer Red ribbon • *Jesse James* (⅝" heart, 1¼" butterfly buttons) • 4 Gold eyelets • Eyelet tools • ⅛" hole punch • E6000 glue

INSTRUCTIONS: **Background:** Cover front of journal with Dominoes paper. Apply ink to edges. • **Mounts:** Glue transparencies in mounts. Back with White cardstock. Mat large mount with torn Red paper. Set eyelets in corners of mounts. Glue mounts to cover. • **Finish:** Cut shanks from buttons. Glue butterfly to large mount and heart to tag. Insert Red thread though tag and tie a knot in ends. Wrap ribbon around journal. Tie a bow.

Friends and family are always traveling and you can be ready with the perfect send-off. Vary your designs and soon you will have a box filled with original cards ready to go at a moment's notice.

Bon Voyage Card
by Lisa Vollrath

MATERIALS: *Design Originals:* Window Card (#0992 Small window); Printed Mount (#0987 Vintage Books); Transparency sheet (#0619 Travel 2) • *Making Memories* Silver star-shaped brads • *Memories* Black dye ink pad • Old postage stamps • *Inkadinkado* Postoid stamps • *Xyron* adhesive • Double sided tape

INSTRUCTIONS: **Card:** Run transparencies through Xyron. Arrange on card as desired. Adhere in place. • **Mount:** Tape Bon Voyage transparency to back of mount. Attach to card over window with brads. • **Finish:** Fill empty spots on card with postage stamps and stamped postoids.

Our Precious Grandchildren

by Diana McMillan

MATERIALS:

Design Originals: Collage paper (#0577 School Days, #0580 School Books); 6 Printed Mounts (#0987 Vintage Books); Transparency sheet (#0624 Art Words) • Cardstock (Red, Black) • Vellum • *Offray* Red ribbon (3 pieces 24" long, 1 piece 30" long) • *ColorBox* Cat's Eye ink (Chestnut Roan, Scarlet) • *WackyTac* Vellum tape • Zots 3-D by *ThermOWeb*

INSTRUCTIONS:

Mats: Cut Black and Red cardstock to fit photo. Layer photo on Red cardstock. Layer matted photo onto Black cardstock. Adhere to page.

Title: Cut out books from School Books paper. Ink edges. Adhere to page with Zots 3-D. • Computer print title on vellum. Tear out words. Adhere to page with vellum tape.

Mounts: Measure and cut 3 slits in fold of 5 mounts. Tape one end of each 24" ribbon and trim to a point. Fold and ink all edges of mounts. Book cover: Adhere transparency and photo into uncut mount for cover. Lay cover flat face down, and adhere untaped ribbon ends to inside of mount, adhere closed. • Adhere all other photos into mounts. • Thread ribbon through slits on printed side of each mount. • Adhere mounts closed. • Accordion fold mounts so transparency is on top. • Attach the center of a 30" ribbon to the back of the bottom mount. • Adhere mount to page. • Tie ribbon ends into a bow.

Family is Forever...

A mini accordion mounted onto a beautiful page is a great way to preserve photos of children and family during the years.

Here's a great idea for those of you looking for clever ways to get more photos on a page. This accordion book holds 11 images.

1. Cut slits in hinges (fold of mount) of each mount.

2. Apply tape to ends of ribbon and cut to a point.

3. Tape ribbon inside the cover mount (1st mount).

4. Thread ribbons through slits. Secure with tape.

Same Paper... 3 Different Ways

by Diana McMillan

Great decorative papers become more versatile when mixed with different colors and embellishments.

It's easy to completely alter the mood of a page and preserve your valuable memories by changing the simple basic elements.

If you've been wondering whether it is "OK" to put large items on your pages, the answer is yes. Objects offer one more way to engage the attention of the viewer.

If you don't like lumpy pages, make a color photocopy to use in place of the real thing.

My Dog... Piper

MATERIALS:

Design Originals: Collage papers (#0583 Stories for Boys, #0584 Puppies at Play); Printed mounts (#0984 Vintage Script); Transparency sheet (#0625 Memories) • *Bazzill* cardstock (Watermelon, Flamingo) • Pink brad • *Nostalgique* letter stickers • Zots 3-D, Mounting Squares by *ThermOWeb*

INSTRUCTIONS:

Background: Cut Watermelon cardstock 11½" x 11½". Adhere to Flamingo background. • Adhere transparency to the corner of the page with vellum tape. • Adhere Puppies paper to Stories paper, making sure the puppies are right side up in the corner that will be turned back. Turn back corner and secure with brad. • **Mat:** Cut mats to fit photo. Adhere photo to mats with Mounting Squares, adhere to page. • **Tags:** Adhere sticker letters to small tags. Adhere to page with Zots 3-D. • Thread ribbon through tag holes. Wrap fibers and tags around page and secure ends to the back of the page.

Orchard in the Fall

MATERIALS:

Design Originals: Collage paper (#0584 Puppies at Play); Printed mounts (#0983 Tapes); Transparency sheets (#0556 Word Tags, #0625 Memories) • Cardstock (Light Green, Dark Green) • Straw mesh • *Xyron* adhesive • Zots 3-D, Memory Tape Runner by *ThermOWeb*

INSTRUCTIONS:

Background: Run mesh through Xyron. Adhere to the bottom of the page. • **Mats:** Cut mats to fit photos. Adhere photo to Dark Green mat. Adhere to Light Green mat with Zots 3-D. Adhere to page. • **Mounts:** Print journaling on Light Green cardstock. Cut to fit small mount. Adhere journaling and transparencies to the back of the mounts. Adhere to page with Zots 3-D.

My Favorite Companions

MATERIALS:

Design Originals: Collage paper (#0584 Puppies at Play); Printed mounts (#0980 Water Marks); Transparency sheets (#0556 Word Tags, #0625 Memories) • *Bazzill* cardstock (Nutmeg, Dark Butter) • Fibers • Memory Tape Runner • Foam Squares

INSTRUCTIONS:

Border: Tear Tan cardstock 5¼" x 12". Tear Nutmeg cardstock 4¾" x 12". Tear Puppies paper 4½" x 8¾". • Adhere Puppies paper to Nutmeg mat. Wrap fibers and tie, secure to back of page. Adhere to Dark Butter mat with foam squares. Adhere to page with foam squares. • **Mat:** Cut Dark Butter and Nutmeg mats to fit photos. Layer and adhere to page with foam squares. • **Mounts:** Adhere transparencies to the back of the mounts. Adhere to page with foam squares.

Wow! Page composition can be so easy, especially when you choose a wonderful decorative paper to set the theme.

These three pages are exactly the same composition... only the decorative paper, colors and embellishment have changed.

Same Layers...
3 Different Papers
by Diana McMillan

Believe In Yourself
MATERIALS:

Design Originals: Collage paper (#0599 Vintage Cards); Printed Mounts (#0983 Tapes); Transparency sheets (#0623 Games, #0624 Art Words) • *Bazzill* cardstock (Raven, Aztec) • *ColorBox* Cat's Eye Orange ink • Black *Magic Mesh* • Magnifying glass • *JudiKins* Diamond Glaze • Mounting Squares, Zots 3-D by *ThermOWeb*

INSTRUCTIONS:

Background: Tear Raven cardstock into 2 pieces 4" x 12" and 6" x 12". Tear Aztec cardstock into 2 pieces 3" x 12" and 5" x 12". • Computer print words onto 3" x 12" Aztec cardstock. • Layer as shown and adhere to page with Zots 3-D. Adhere 3" x 12" strip of Black mesh to page. • **Mounts**: Adhere photos and transparencies to mounts, adhere to page with Zots 3-D. • **Finish**: Adhere magnifying glass with Diamond Glaze.

My Sister, My Friend
MATERIALS:

Design Originals : Collage paper (#0586 Vintage Flowers); Printed Mounts (#0984 Vintage Script); Transparency sheet (#0622 Beauties) • *Bazzill* cardstock (Flamingo, Watermelon) • Pink *Magic Mesh* • *Hirschberg Schutz* dress • Mounting Squares, Zots 3-D by *ThermOWeb*

INSTRUCTIONS:

Background: Tear Flamingo cardstock into 2 pieces 4" x 12" and 6" x 12". Tear Watermelon cardstock into 2 pieces 3" x 12" and 5" x 12". • Computer print words onto 3" x 12" Watermelon cardstock. • Layer as shown and adhere to page with Zots 3-D. Adhere 3" x 12" strip of Pink mesh to page. • **Mounts**: Adhere photos and transparencies to mounts, adhere to page with Zots 3-D. • **Finish**: Adhere dress to page with Zots 3-D.

Catch of the Day
MATERIALS:

Design Originals: Collage paper (#0581 Little Boys, #0605 Deep Sea); Printed Mount (#0981 Diamonds); Transparency sheets (#0620 Seaside, #0624 Art Words) • *Bazzill* cardstock (Dark Butter, Ivory) • *ColorBox* Cat's Eye Ochre ink • Beige *Magic Mesh* • 3 jump rings • Twine or string • Twig • *JudiKins* Diamond Glaze • Mounting Squares, Zots 3-D by *ThermOWeb*

INSTRUCTIONS:

Background: Tear Ivory cardstock into 2 pieces 4" x 12" and 6" x 12". Tear Dark Butter cardstock into 2 pieces 3" x 12" and 5" x 12". • Computer print words onto 3" x 12" Dark Butter cardstock. • Layer as shown and adhere to page with Zots 3-D. Adhere 3" x 12" strip of Beige mesh to page. • **Mounts**: Adhere photos and transparencies to mounts, adhere to page with Zots 3-D. • **Finish**: Cut out fish from Deep Sea paper. Insert jump rings in fish mouths. Wrap twill around twig. Tie end of twine to jump rings. Adhere twig with Diamond Glaze. Adhere fish with foam squares.

Scrapbook Pages on the Wall

Make a wall layout with your favorite scrapbook pages so your family can enjoy precious memories all year long. At the end of the year, just slide the pages into your scrapbook! I hope these projects give you fresh new ideas.

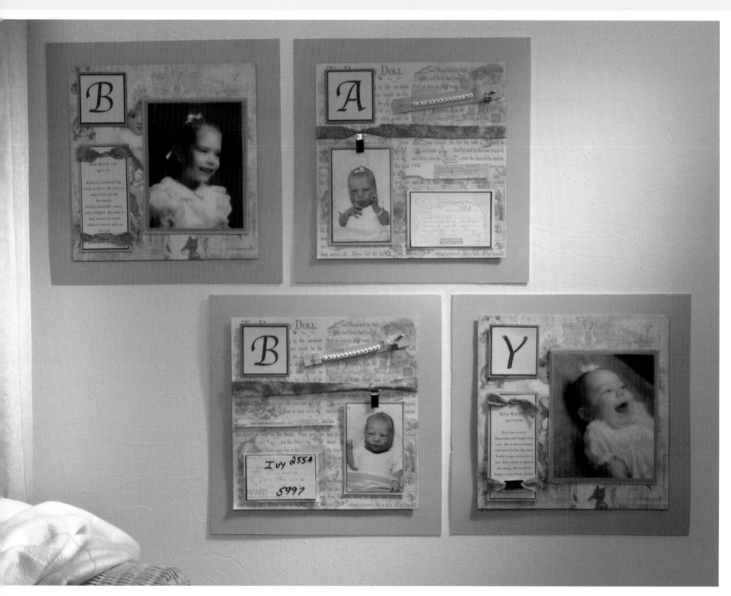

'B-A-B-Y'... Our Baby Girls

by Kim Ivy

MATERIALS:

Design Originals: Collage paper (2 each of #0585 Little Girls, #0587 Runaway Doll) • *Bazzill* cardstock (2 each of Flamingo, Raven, Watermelon) • Letter beads • Silver tags (spirit, joy, imagine, dream) • 2 Silver jump rings • 4 large stick pins • Fabric scrap • *Dritz* suspender clip • ¼" hole punch • Foam tape • Adhesive

INSTRUCTIONS:

Letter blocks are the same for all 4 pages. Print letter on Flamingo cardstock. Mat with Raven and Watermelon. Layer and glue mats together. Adhere to page with foam tape.

Layouts "A" and "B" are assembled the same way.

Background: Adhere memorabilia to page with foam tape. • **Title**: Tear a piece of Watermelon cardstock ¾" x 7½". Poke pin through paper. Spell name out with baby beads and string onto pins. Adhere to page with foam tape. Attach word tag to pin with jump ring. **Mat**: Double-mat photo with Raven and Watermelon cardstock. Adhere to Runaway Doll paper with foam tape. • Mat hospi-

tal tag with Raven and Flamingo cardstock. Adhere to page. • **Finish**: Tear fabric into 1" wide strips. Tie suspender clip to fabric. Wrap fabric to the back of the page and secure. Clip to photo. • Print large "B" on Flamingo cardstock. Mat with Raven and Watermelon. Layer and glue together. Adhere to page with foam tape.

Layouts "B" and "Y" are assembled the same way. **Mat**: Double-mat photo with Flamingo and Watermelon cardstock. Glue to Little Girls paper. • **Finish**: Print Journaling on Flamingo cardstock. Double-mat with Raven and Watermelon cardstock. Punch 2 holes in the top. Push a bit of fabric through each hole. Tape to the back of the mat. • Thread fabric strips through the holes in the word tag. Wrap around cardstock. Tape to the back of the mat. Adhere tag to mat with foam tape. • Adhere to page with foam tape.

MOUNT PAGES FOR THE WALL:

At the frame shop, I chose pink matboard to mount the pages. The shop cut the matboard so all I had to do was attach the pages with foam tape.

Dedicate a shadow box to the memory of some-one you love. Collect and preserve special memorabilia that had meaning to that individual. This is a good place to add a personal touch with journaling.

Shadow Box

by Kim Ivy

MATERIALS:

Design Originals: Collage paper (#0586 Vintage Flowers); Printed Mounts (#0983 Tapes); Transparency sheet (#0625 Memories) • Shadow box • Personal memorabilia (Antique buttons, rosary, doily, prayer book) • *Li'l Davis* key • *Dumblebeasts* stickers (Sewing machine, Scissors, Pincushion) • *Die Cuts* Metallic Accents letter tags • 2 *Collage Keepsakes* Silver photo frames • *Making Memories* (word ribbon, safety pins) • 1903 house numbers • Drill • Small drill bit • Wire • Foam tape • Adhesive

INSTRUCTIONS:

Background: Cut Vintage Flowers paper to fit the bottom of the box. Position ribbon and tape to the back of the page. Add safety pins and tags for title. Glue images of sewing tools in position. • **Embellishments**: Adhere photos to the openings in the house numbers, mounts and frames. Glue numbers in place. Adhere doily and key in place. • **Mounts**: Adhere mounts with foam tape. Glue buttons to mount corners. • **Finish**: Drill a small hole in the top of the box. Wire rosary in position. Add prayer book. Close the box.

Erin, Tessa, and Doug

by Diana McMillan

MATERIALS FOR EACH PAGE:

Design Originals: Collage paper (#0579 ABCs Dictionary, #0484 Blue Linen); Printed Mounts (#0986 Color Game, #0987 Vintage Books) • Manila cardstock • 4 Black photo corners • Gold charm • 'Fairfield' computer font • Zots 3-D, Mounting Squares by *ThermOWeb*

INSTRUCTIONS: **Mat**: Cut Blue Linen paper mat for photo. Add photo corners. Adhere photo to mat with mounting squares. Adhere to page with Zots 3-D. • **Mounts**: Adhere mounts to top of page with Zots 3-D. • Computer print letters and journaling on cardstock. Cut out letters and journal box. • Tape journal box to the back of the large mount. Adhere charm to bottom of mount with Zots 3-D. • **Title**: Adhere letters to mounts with Zots 3-D.

1. Punch petals from 4 colors of cardstock and Vellum. Layer colors for a flower.

2. Top off with a Pink flower.

3. Glue buttons in place.

Frame a Transparency of a vintage photo in a slide mount for a beautiful look

Sugar and Spice
by Delores Frantz

Pink is the perfect color to express the "sugar and spice" that little girls are made of. Combine two related decorative papers to create a great look. Repeat the white from a photo into the layout with a grosgrain ribbon in the center of a cardstock border.

MATERIALS:
Design Originals: Collage papers (#0585 Little Girls, #0586 Vintage Flowers, #0587 Runaway Doll, #0588 Kittens At Play, #0607 Vellum Sentiments); Mounts (#0988 Small White, #0991 Large White); Transparency sheet (#0621 Children) • *ColorBox* Cat's Eye Warm Red ink • 13" of Ivory 1" grosgrain ribbon • *Jesse James* 1½" heart charm • 10 Black eyelets • ⅛" hole punch • Eyelet tools • Adhesive • Foam squares

INSTRUCTIONS:
Border: Tear a strip of Runaway doll 3½" x 12" and a strip of Kittens At Play 2½" x 12". Ink torn edges. • Stack strips and glue to the left side of Flower paper. Glue ribbon down center of paper strips. • **Mounts:** Cover small mounts with Flower paper and large mount with Kitten paper. Ink the edges. • Glue transparencies in small mounts. Attach to ribbon with eyelets. • Glue Vellum sentiment to large mount. Glue to page. • **Mat** photo on torn Kitten paper. Apply ink to edges. Attach photo to page with eyelets. • **Finish:** Glue heart at top. Tear girl image from Little Girl paper. Ink the edges. Attach to page with foam squares.

String word beads across the center border

Add the page title with a small note in a vellum envelope

1. Tear the edges of decorative paper.

2. Age the edges with chalk ink.

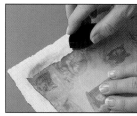

3. Dab the edges with chalk ink farther in.

Sugar, spice, everything nice...and pink!.
Use beautiful Vintage Flowers paper to complement a pink baby dress.
Along with soft pastel colors ,beautiful embellishments and layered flowers,
this combination creates an 'all girl' feminine layout.

Daddy's Little Girl - Sweet Princess

by Christy Gilbreath

MATERIALS:

Design Originals: Collage papers (#0585 Little Girls, #0586 Vintage Flowers); Mount (#0991 Large White); Transparency sheet (#0621 Children) • *Bazzill* cardstock (Chiffon, Lemonade, Leap Frog, Blossom, Flamingo) • *Magnetic Poetry* Pink word beads • 1 Gold safety pin • *Renaissance Art* Art Keepers glass charm • Yellow fibers • *Offray* sheer Pink ribbon • Vellum (1 Pink envelope, 1 White rectangle) • *EK Success* Daisy punch • ¼" buttons (4 White, 5 Yellow) • 2 White 1" heart button • *JudiKins* Diamond Glaze • Vellum tape • Red Liner tape

DADDY'S LITTLE GIRL PAGE:

Background: Trim Chiffon cardstock to 11½" x 11½". Glue to Lemonade cardstock. Tear a strip of Leap Frog ¾" x 12". Glue to page on the diagonal. Tear 2 pieces of Vintage Flowers paper as shown. Glue to page. • **Mat**: Cut a Lemonade mat to fit the photo. Glue to page. • **Title**: Print on vellum. Cut to size. Mat with Lemonade cardstock with vellum tape. • **Finish**: Glue ribbon, buttons, and title in place. • Punch flowers: 2 Blossom, 1 Flamingo, 1 Vellum. Layer Blossom-Flamingo-Vellum-Pink. Glue to page. Adhere small buttons with Diamond Glaze.

SWEET PRINCESS PAGE:

Background: Tear Chiffon cardstock 3¾" x 12" and 7" x 12". Glue to Lemonade as shown. • **Border**: Tear a strip of Leap Frog cardstock 1⅞" x 12" and a strip of Vintage Flowers 1¼" x 12". Glue in place. • Thread floss through word beads. Adhere beads with Diamond Glaze. Attach safety pin to page. • **Mounts**: Cut mount apart at hinge. Cover with Vintage Flowers paper. Adhere transparencies to the back of the mounts. Adhere mounts to page. • **Charm**: Cut out image of girl from Little Girls paper. Assemble charm. Adhere to page with Diamond Glaze. Thread ribbon through charm and safety pin. Tie a bow. • **Finish**: • Punch flowers: 1 Blossom, 1 Flamingo, 1 Leap Frog. Layer Leap Frog-Flamingo-Blossom. Glue to page. Adhere small buttons with Diamond Glaze. Cut out a flower from Vintage Flowers paper. Glue in place. • Adhere Vellum envelope to page with Vellum tape. Print message on Vellum. Cut to size. Insert into envelope. Adhere pendant to page with Diamond Glaze.

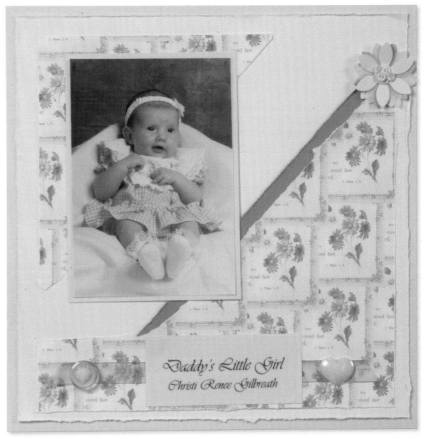

Diana
by Diana McMillan

For appealing pages every time, use the colors in the photo to determine the colors of your page composition.

MATERIALS:
Design Originals: Collage paper (#0586 Vintage Flowers, #0566 Music); Mounts (#0988 Small White, #0991 Large White); Transparency sheet (#0621 Children) • Cardstock (Green, Pink) • *Offray* Pink ribbon • *Boxer* mini brads (5 Pink, 1 Gold) • *7gypsies* 4 Gold photo corners • 1 Pink flower • *Nostalgiques* Tea Stained Tag ABC stickers • 1 small Manila tag • 1 Gold charm • Memory Tape Runner

INSTRUCTIONS:
Mat: Cut Pink and Green cardstock mats. Adhere photo to Pink mat. Wrap ribbon as shown. Thread charm and tag. Tie a bow. Mat onto Green cardstock. Adhere to page. • **Mounts**: Cover mounts with Music paper. Adhere transparencies to the back of the mounts. • Add corners, flower, and ribbon to large mount. Attach ribbon to page with Gold brad. Adhere small mounts in place. • **Title**: Cut a piece of Green cardstock to fit title. Add stickers and brads, adhere to page.

Helpful Hints
Stiffening the end of a thread, cord or fiber will make it much easier to thread thru the hole in a tag, bead or ring.

Dip the end of fiber in glue. Twist the ends. Let dry.

Or, wrap fiber ends with a pointed spiral of masking tape.

Or, make a needle threader with a 4" length of bent wire.

1. Glue paper to front of mount. Let dry.

2. Cut out window. Cut corners at an angle.

3. Attach a transparency or photo to mount.

4. Wrap and glue paper to back of mount.

Diana and Jodi
by Diana McMillan

MATERIALS:

Design Originals: Collage paper (#0585 Little Girls); Printed Mount (#0984 Vintage Script); Transparency sheet (#0622 Beauties) • Cardstock (Rose, White) • Vellum • 3 *Demis Products* Gold hinges • 2 Gold photo corners • 1 Gold bookplate • *ColorBox* Cat's Eye ink (Burnt Copper, Dusty Plum, Old Rose) • *JudiKins* Diamond Glaze • Zots 3-D, Mounting Squares by *ThermOWeb*

INSTRUCTIONS: .

Mats: Adhere Rose cardstock to back of Little Girls paper and ink edges with Burnt Copper. Determine position of photo and tear a hole through both papers. Ink and curl back edges of hole. • Adhere photo behind torn hole. • Glue to White background for stability. • **Title**: Print title on Vellum. Cut out and adhere inside bookplate. Adhere to page with Diamond Glaze. **Mounts**: Ink front and edges of mounts with Burnt Copper. Cut each small mount diagonally in one corner. Intertwine mounts. Tape the back of the mounts to hold them in position. Adhere transparencies to the back of mounts. • Adhere photo corners over cut corners with Diamond Glaze. Adhere mounts to page with Zots 3-D. • **Finish**: Attach hinges to the side of the page with Diamond Glaze.

Little Jodi Sue
by Diana McMillan

Relive the precious moments of your child's life when you make a page full of spirited moments and hopeful expressions.

MATERIALS:

Design Originals: Collage paper (#0588 Kittens at Play, #0608 Vellum Shorthand) • Printed Mount (#0981 Diamonds) • Transparency sheet (#0556 Word Tags) • Cardstock (Pink, Rose, Turquoise) • Pink *Magic Mesh* • 2 Turquoise heart beads • Turquoise letter beads for name • Fibers (Turquoise, Pink) • Zots 3-D, Mounting Squares by *ThermOWeb* • *WackyTac* Vellum tape

INSTRUCTIONS: **Background**: Cut 2 pieces of mesh 1" x 12". Cut 1 piece of mesh 2½" x 6". Adhere mesh as shown in photo. • **Borders**: Tear 6" x 12" Rose and 5½" x 12" Pink strips. Layer and adhere to page with Zots 3-D. • **Mounts**: Adhere photos and transparency words to the back of /74120mounts. Adhere mounts and beads to page with Zots 3-D. • **Mat photo** with Rose and Turquoise cardstock. Add photo to bottom corner with Zots 3-D. • **Title**: Tear vellum. Tape to page. • String name beads on fibers, adhere to page with Zots 3-D.

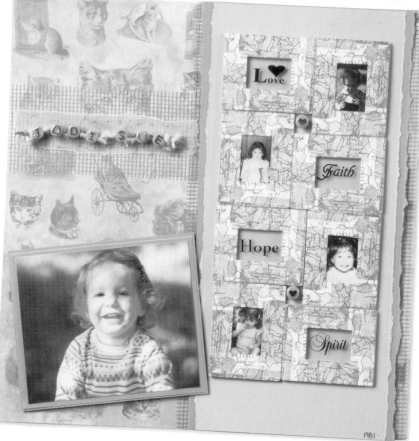

MATERIALS:
Design Originals: Collage papers (#0587 The Runaway Doll, #0588 Kittens at Play) • Red cardstock • *Offray* ribbons (36" of ⅜" wide Gold, 12" of 1" wide sheer Apricot) • *Lara's* Wood tags • *ColorBox* Cat's Eye ink (Chestnut Roan, Gold Rush) • *7gypsies* Walnut Ink • Super Tape, Foam squares, Memory Tape Runner by *ThermOWeb*

INSTRUCTIONS:
Background: Crumple 8" square of Red paper and age with Gold ink. • Tear 6" x 8" piece of Runaway Doll paper and age edges with Chestnut Roan. Apply a wash of Walnut ink to Kittens paper. • **Assembly**: Adhere papers and photo as shown. • Apply Super tape to edge of photo. Remove tape backing. Zig-zag fold the ribbon, adhering to tape as you go. Add bow. • **Title**: Age wood tags with Chestnut Roan. Adhere to page with foam squares.

How to Make 'Ruched' Ribbon

Hannah
by Stephanie Greenwood

Paper choices and arrangement of page elements convey a subliminal meaning. This baby looks like a treasured package that has just been unwrapped. What a wonderfully powerful, positive message!

1. Apply Super Tape around the edge of your photo. Remove paper lining.

2. Zig-zag fold ribbon in a 'ruching' pattern, adhering ribbon to tape as you go.

How to Make Crumpled Metallic Paper

1. Wet paper. Crumple the paper well with your hands. Flatten paper. Let dry.

2. Apply metallic ink with Gold Rush. Let dry.

MATERIALS:
Design Originals: Collage paper (#0587 Runaway Doll); Printed Mount (#0985 Dictionary); Transparency sheet (#0621 Children) • Rose Cardstock • 6 Rose eyelets • *Krylon* Gold Metallic pen • *Adornaments* fibers • *EK Success* Corner Adorner punches (Wrought Iron, Iron Eagle) • *Qwik Cuts* letter die • Zots 3-D • ClicknStick Mounting Tabs

INSTRUCTIONS:

Background: Tear Runaway Doll paper and glue to Rose cardstock. Set eyelets. Lace fibers. • **Mounts:** Adhere transparency images to the back of the mounts. Adhere to page with Zots 3-D. • **Mat:** Punch corners. Mat photo onto Rose cardstock. Adhere photo mat in place. **Title:** Cut out letters. Ink edges with Krylon pen. Adhere to page.

Amy Joy
by Diana McMillan

This is an excellent example of exquisite results using simple techniques. The elements on the page are few in number. The beauty of this page comes from an expertly chosen color scheme and carefully selected embellishments.

The rose colors throughout the page match the subtle colors in the photograph. The fibers are similar to the colors of the photo and background paper. The transparencies and mounts extend the theme.

How to Make Punch Entwined Corners

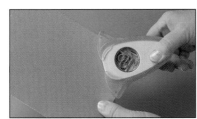

1. Hold the punch upside down so you can see the corner. Punch corner with first punch.

2. Punch corner with second punch.

3. Insert photo.

Blue and brown... the perfect color for boys of all ages. Choose decorative papers to preserve your valuable memories, then add colored cardstock to finish the page. Nostalgic decorative papers make these pages easy.

Tatom

by Kim Ivy

Blue borders accented with twill tape and game pieces build dimension into this well-balanced layout. Metal brads, wood game pieces and brown papers complement this masculine theme.

MATERIALS:

Design Originals: Collage paper (#0583 Stories for Boys, #0488 Rust Stripe); Mounts (#0991 Large White); Transparency sheet (#0561 Travel) • *Bazzill* Typhoon cardstock • 4 Gold brads • 2 pieces of latch hook rug binding 1¼" x 11" • 2 pieces of *Wright's* twill ribbon (½" x 3½")• *ColorBox* Cat's Eye Chestnut Roan Ink • *Li'l Davis* letter tiles • Fine grit sandpaper • Adhesive • Foam tape

INSTRUCTIONS:

Mat: Cut Rust Stripe paper to mat photo. Sand the edges. Adhere photo to mat. Adhere to Stories for Boys paper. • **Mount**: Cut mount apart at hinge. Cover with Rust Stripe paper. Scuff with sandpaper. Attach transparency. Add twill ribbons with brads. Adhere mount with foam tape. • **Borders**: Tear Blue cardstock and adhere to the top and bottom of the page. • Adhere twill with foam tape. • **Title**: Adhere wood tiles to page with foam tape.

HELPFUL HINT:
To keep a scrapbook page from being lumpy, you can color copy the game pieces then glue the flat pieces on the twill tape instead of bulky wooden pieces.

How to Unravel the Ends of Twill Tape

1. Unravel the ends of tape with a T-pin or needle.

2. Glue game pieces to twill tape for the title.

To Swim or Not To Swim

by Diana McMillan

This stunning page is a breeze to make. Simply tear two shades of blue cardstock into border strips. Position them on top of Blue mesh. Top the border strips with printed mounts filled with memorable words and images on top of the border strips.

Make your title stand out with shadow letters on foam squares.

MATERIALS:

Design Originals: Collage paper (#0583 Stories for Boys); Printed Mounts (#0982 Game Pieces, #0983 Tapes); Transparency sheets (#0557 Family, #0559 Alphabet, #0560 Objects, #0562 Nature) • Cardstock (Light and Dark Blue) • *ColorBox* Cat's Eye ink (Light Blue, Dark Blue) • *Magic Mesh* Blue Dottie Ann mesh • 20 Blue eyelets • *Dayco* Bitty letter dies • Eyelet tools • Foam squares

INSTRUCTIONS:

Borders: Cut 4 strips of mesh 1" x 12". Tear cardstock. Ink the edges. Adhere mesh to each side of page. Layer and adhere to mesh with foam squares. • **Mounts**: Adhere transparencies to mounts. Set eyelets. Adhere to pages with foam tape.

Mats: Cut Dark Blue cardstock. Ink the edges. Adhere photo to mat. Cut Light Blue cardstock and ink the edges and adhere below photo for journaling. Adhere mats to page with foam squares.

Title: Cut out and assemble letters. Adhere to page with foam squares.

How to Mount a Transparency

1. Punch holes with an eyelet punch tool, a hammer and a protective pad for your table.

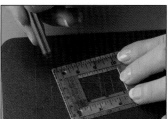

2. Set eyelets with an eyelet setter tool and a hammer. If an eyelet is too short to go through a mount, simply add a dot of glue to secure it in the hole.

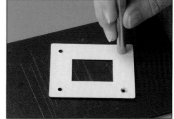

3. Adhere a transparency image inside of a mount.

Jason

by Delores Frantz

Grosgrain ribbon, a small buckle and three eyelets make an interesting base for a title. Three layers of blending decorative papers build interest in the background while the corrugated paper mat draws attention to the photo.

Top the page off with a title made with transparent letters... you can see the beautiful decorative paper behind. Frame a nostalgic saying on Vellum in a large slide mount.

MATERIALS:
Design Originals: Collage papers (#0581 Little Boys, #0582 Toys for Boys, #0583 Stories for Boys, #0607 Vellum Sentiments); Mounts (#0988 Small White, #0991 Large White); Transparency sheet (#0559 Alphabet) • Crimped Brown craft paper • *ColorBox* Cat's Eye Chestnut Roan ink • 14" Black ⅜" grosgrain ribbon • *Dritz* Fray Check • *Making Memories* (⅞" buckle, 4 photo corners) • 12 Antique Silver eyelets • ⅛" hole punch • Eyelet tools • Adhesive • *JudiKins* Diamond Glaze

INSTRUCTIONS:
Background: Tear a strip of Stories paper 3" x 12" and a strip of Toys paper 5½" x 12". Apply ink to edges. Layer strips and glue across Boys paper. • **Mat** photo on crimped Brown paper. Glue metal corners to mat. • **Ribbon**: Cut ribbon to a point. Use Fray Check on raw edges. Set 3 eyelets near point. Slide on buckle and glue ribbon across bottom of page. • **Mounts**: Cover large mount with Toys paper and small mounts with Stories paper. Apply ink to edges. Adhere Vellum saying in large mount and letters in small mounts. Attach to page with eyelets.

Secure Transparencies in Mounts

1. Cover mounts with decorative papers (see page 12). Age the edges of mounts with *Cat's Eye* chalk ink.

2. Cut an image or letter from a Transparency sheet. Tape the transparency to the back of a mount.

We have many photos of the rough-and-tumble moments our sons have. Balance those with some pages of tender moments. This page captures the tender while preserving the masculine tone with colors and fibers that say "all boy".

friend - one who cherishes kind regard for another person

There's no love like the love between a boy and his dog. -DAP

How to Secure Twine

1. Punch two holes in a mount. Push twine through the hole.

2. Tie a knot to secure the twine.

A Boy and His Dog
by Diana McMillan

Set the stage to show off your best friend with nostalgic themed background papers.

MATERIALS:
Design Originals: Collage papers (#0583 Stories for Boys, #0584 Puppies at Play, #0493 Brown Linen); Printed Mount (#0981 Diamonds) • Vellum • *7gypsies* word ribbon • Twine • 2 *Boxer* Black mini brads• ¼" hole punch • Zots 3-D by *ThermOWeb*

INSTRUCTIONS:
Background: Tear Puppies paper and adhere to Stories paper. • **Title**: Computer print words on Vellum. Let it dry. Tear the bottom edge. Attach to page with brads. • **Mat** photo with Brown Linen and glue to page. • **Mount**: Adhere photo to the mount. • Punch holes in mount. Thread twine and ribbon through the holes and tie a knot. Adhere mount to page with Zots 3-D. Secure ribbon and twine to the back of the page.

Create attractive masculine pages with wood grains, corrugated textures and papers designed for boys. Your young men will love looking at these pages, and you will have fun sharing them with your grandchildren too.

Sweet Feet
by Delores Frantz

MATERIALS:

Design Originals: Collage paper (#0581 Little Boys, #0608 Vellum Shorthand, #0481 Teal Linen); Printed Mounts (#0982 Game Pieces, #0983 Tapes); Transparency sheet (#0621 Children) • Crimped Brown corrugated craft paper 5½" x 8½" • White cardstock • *Remember When* ⅝" Black 3-D letters • 12" of Black 1mm cord • *Jesse James* ⅝" Silver heart buttons • Silver eyelets (4 square ⅜", 9 round) • ⅛" hole punch • Eyelet tools • *JudiKins* Diamond Glaze• E6000

INSTRUCTIONS:

Background: Tear a 7" x 12" piece of vellum. Place on Little Boys paper. Center craft paper on vellum. Attach both to Little Boys paper with square eyelets. Tie cord through top eyelets. • **Mat:** Cut Teal mat to fit photo, adhere to page. • **Mounts**: Adhere transparencies in mounts. Back with White cardstock. Adhere to page. • **Title**: Attach tags across top of page with eyelets. Glue letters to tags. Cut shanks from heart buttons. Glue to mounts with E6000.

Puppy Kisses
by Diana McMillan

MATERIALS:

Design Originals: Collage paper (#0581 Little Boys); Printed mounts (#0980 Water Marks); Transparency sheet (#0621 Children) • *Bazzill* cardstock (Walnut, Bark) • 4 Black photo corners • 7 Red eyelets • Eyelet tools • Mounting Squares • Zots 3-D

INSTRUCTIONS:

Border: Tear Bark cardstock 5" x 12". Tear Walnut cardstock 4½" x 12". Stack and adhere to page with Zots 3-D. • **Mat**: Tear Bark mat 2½" x 4". Tear Walnut journal box 2" x 3½". Record journaling. Set eyelets. Adhere to page with Zots 3-D. • **Mount**: Adhere transparency to the back of the mount. Adhere to page with Zots 3-D. • **Finish**: Place photo corners on photo and adhere to page with Zots 3-D.

RJ Smiles
by Diana McMillan

Really Quick, Very Easy! And fun to do. The colors in the photo, mats and mounts work together. Cutting out the elements in the background paper adds dimension and interest.

MATERIALS:

Design Originals: Collage paper (#0582 Toys for Boys); Printed Mounts (#0986 Color Game); Transparency sheets (#0559 Alphabet, #0625 Memories) • Cardstock (Red, Blue) • *ColorBox* Cat's Eye ink (Royal Blue, Scarlet) • Scrap of Vellum • Black marker • Adhesive • Zots 3-D • *WackyTac* Vellum tape

INSTRUCTIONS:

Background: Tear Toys for Boys paper 7¾" x 12". Ink the edges. Adhere to Red cardstock. • **Mat**: Cut Blue and Red mat for photo. Ink the edges. Adhere transparency letters and photo to mat. Adhere Blue mat to Red mat and then to page with Zots 3-D. • **Mounts**: Print journaling on Vellum. Tape Vellum and transparencies to the back of the mounts. Adhere to page with Zots 3-D. • **Finish**: Cut out 2 airplanes on the Toys for Boys paper. Trace around edges with a marker. Adhere to page with Zots 3-D.

1. Cut out an object from Toys decorative paper.

2. Trace around the edge of the object with a marker.

3. Secure the object to the page with Zots 3-D.

The first day of school brings so many critical decisions. This page captures Jodi's "what to wear" dilemma.

First Day of School
by Diana McMillan

Here's Luke, looking happy and self assured on his first day. Special events deserve a page all their own.

MATERIALS:

Design Originals: Collage paper (#0577 School Days, #0578 Vintage ABCs, #0579 ABCs Dictionary, #0580 School Books) • Cardstock (Red, Blue) • *The Bead Shop* Letter beads • *ColorBox* Cat's Eye ink (Colonial Blue, Frost White) • *JudiKins* Diamond Glaze • Adhesive • Foam Squares

INSTRUCTIONS:

Background: Cut ABCs Dictionary paper 5" x 12". Glue to top of School Days paper. • **Paper Ribbon:** Cut a strip of Red cardstock 1" x 12". Adhere to page with foam squares. Cut a strip of Red ¹/4" x 12" to fit the back of the beads. String beads onto Red strip. Adhere strip in place. • **Mat:** Adhere photo to Blue cardstock mat. • Cut School Books paper to make a larger mat. Sand and ink the edges. Cut Red cardstock ¹/2" larger. • Adhere School Books paper to Red cardstock. • Adhere photo mat to School Books mat with foam squares. Adhere to page with foam squares. • **Title**: Cut letters from Vintage ABCs paper. Cut Red cardstock ¹/4" larger. Ink the edges of Red cardstock with White Frost. Glue letters to Red mats. Adhere to page with foam squares.

To get the dimensional effect in the title, use 2 layers of foam squares on every other letter.

Age the edges of wood, paper or plastic letter tiles with *Cat's Eye* chalk inks.

These multi-layer side borders direct your attention to the center of the page, making your photos the main attraction. For a quick and easy frame that adds color and focus, mat your photo in a printed mount.

School Days

School Days

by Diana McMillan

on page 22

MATERIALS:

Design Originals: Collage paper (#0577 School Days); Printed Mounts (#0987 Vintage Books); Cardstock (Red, Black) • Vellum • 3 Black brads • 6 Black eyelets • *DMC* Black floss • *Li'l Davis* letter tiles • *ColorBox* Cat's Eye Scarlet ink • Eyelet tools • Mounting Squares • Zots 3-D

INSTRUCTIONS:

Background: Tear Black cardstock 5⅜" x 12" and 1⅞" x 12". • Tear School Days paper 5" x 12" and 1⅝" x 12". Adhere to Red cardstock as shown. • **Mounts**: Computer print journaling on Vellum. Cut vellum to fit mount. Adhere photos and Vellum to the back of the mounts. • Set eyelets. Position brads. String floss through eyelets and tie knots. Attach to brads. Adhere mounts to page with Zots 3-D. • **Title**: Ink tiles. Adhere tiles to the page with Zots 3-D.

Alphabet

by Delores Frantz

Three layers of torn cardstock define both border areas and focus attention on the center stage of this layout... the fun photos. Tear another strip of ABCDE to tell the story. Center this layer on the left side of the page.

Finish the page with metal stars and a "school days" apple shaker box.

MATERIALS:

Design Originals: Collage papers (# 0578 Vintage ABCs, #0579 ABCs Dictionary); Printed Mounts (#0986 Color Game) • Cardstock (Black, Blue, Red) • Six ⅞" star brads • *Making Memories* eyelet quote • *EK Success* Movers and Shakers Apple • *ColorBox* Cat's Eye Chestnut Roan ink • Eyelet tools • ⅛" hole punch • Adhesive • Foam squares

INSTRUCTIONS:

Background: Tear the following strips: Black 2½" x 12" and 4½" x 12"; Red 2¼" x 12" and 4¼" x 12"; Blue 2" x 12" and 4" x 12"; Vintage ABCs 2¼" x 12". Ink all torn edges. • Layer and adhere strips to ABCs Dictionary paper. • **Mounts**: Adhere photos in mounts and mat with Black cardstock. Adhere to page. • **Finish**: Set eyelet Quote. Attach apple and star brads.

Senior Year
by Diana McMillan

This page demonstrates a great idea to collect all your friends' photos on one page... showcased in individual mounts.

MATERIALS:
Design Originals: Legacy paper (#0484 Blue Linen); Printed Mounts (#0987 Vintage Books); Transparency sheet (#0559 Alphabet) • Scrap of Ivory cardstock • *Boxer* Copper mini brads • *Adornaments* fibers • 1 Nickel star nailhead • Mounting Squares • Zots 3-D

INSTRUCTIONS:
Large Mounts: Cut Ivory name tags to fit in the corner of the mount. Write names. Attach with brads. • Adhere photos to the back of mounts. • Adhere to Blue Linen with Zots 3-D. • **Small Mounts**: Cut out transparency letters. • Adhere letters to the back of the mounts. • Adhere with Zots 3-D. • **Fibers**: Secure fibers to the back of the page. Add star nailhead.

Attach ID Tags to Mounts with Brads

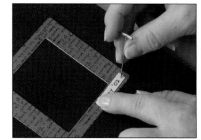

1. Place each mount on a push pad. Use a T-pin to make a hole.

2. Add a brad on each side of the identification tag to secure.

For some reason it is always hard for our teenagers to understand that we were also young once. Help bridge that gap by sharing your school pictures with them. If you have the photos, make a page for each generation. It is so much fun to compare hair styles and clothing...and report cards!

1979

by Christy Gilbreath

This is a great idea to collect all your friends photos... in a bright envelope or pocket.

MATERIALS:

Design Originals: Collage papers (#0578 Vintage ABCs, #0580 School Books) • Cardstock (Blue, Orange, Green) • *Chatterbox* snaps • *Boxer* mini brads • *Making Memories* label holder • *ColorBox* Cat's Eye ink (Brown, Gray) • 1 envelope • 1 paper clip • Old report card • Twine (Green, Blue, Tan) • Adhesive

INSTRUCTIONS:

Background: Ink edges of envelope with Gray. Glue to page. • **Pocket**: Tear Orange paper 3" x 10". Crumple and lay flat. Ink edges and some of the creases. Print label. Cut out "H" from Vintage ABCs paper. Glue to pocket. Attach label holder with brads. Make a "Year" label from Green cardstock to fit the label holder. Attach pocket to page with snaps. • Place old report card into pocket. Paper clip to envelope. • **Mat**: Mat photo with Blue cardstock. Wrap twine around mat and photo. Tie a knot. Glue to page.

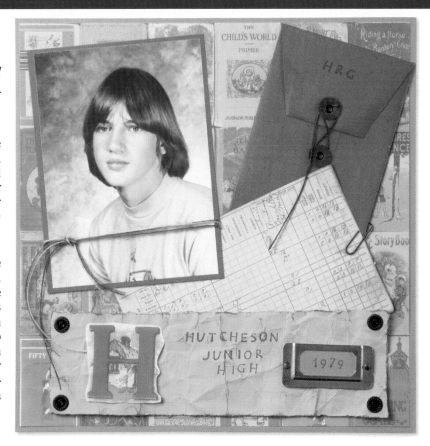

Read Me A Story

by Delores Frantz

Story time is a favorite of many children. Revive fond memories and pass a legacy of literacy down through the generations with scrapbook pages that show people reading and being read to.

MATERIALS:

Design Originals: Collage papers (#0577 School Days, #0579 ABCs Dictionary, #0580 School Books, #0547 Dictionary) • Transparency sheet (#0625 Memories) • Cardstock (Black, White) • *ColorBox* Cat's Eye Chestnut Roan ink • 16 Black eyelets • ⅛" hole punch • Eyelet tools • Adhesive

INSTRUCTIONS:

Title: Tear a piece of Dictionary paper 4" x 11". Ink the edges. Mat on Black cardstock and glue to top of School Books paper. • Cut letters from ABCs paper, mat on Black cardstock and attach to Dictionary paper with eyelets. • **Mats**: Cut large book from School Days paper and apply ink to edges. Mat book and photos on Black cardstock. Arrange on page. • **Finish**: Back transparency with White cardstock. Attach to page with eyelets.

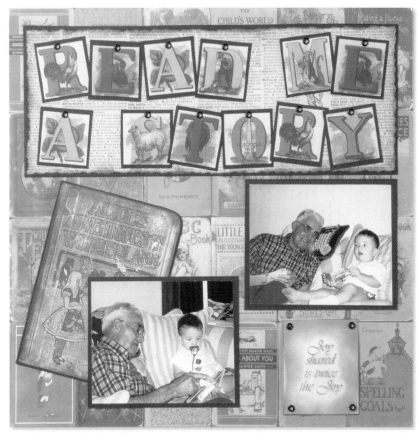

Add Beads

1. Tear Tan cardstock.

2. Add glue along edge.

3. Sprinkle beads on wet glue. Let dry.

Life's A Beach
by Mary Kaye Seckler

"Life's A Beach" is a good example of creating layers of texture. This page really feels like a beach. The crinkled paper makes great sand while fibers reminiscent of seaweed meet waves of torn vellum. Even the sea foam is present in the tiny pearl beads.

This page is so beautiful you will be tempted to hang it in your home.

MATERIALS:
Design Originals: Collage paper (#0590 Seashells); Mounts (#0990 Round White); Transparency sheet (#0620 Seaside) • Cardstock (Dark Blue, Light Blue, Tan) • Vellum • Tan handmade paper • 5 small metal round tags • 4 Turquoise ⅛" eyelets • ¼" eyelets (4 Blue, 6 Silver) • Pearl glass beads • *JudiKins* (Diamond Glaze, Swirl background stamp) • *Sharon Soneff* Faux Wax Seals • *Sonnets* Blueberry Sorbet Alphadots Stickers • Blue *Craf-T* Decorating Chalk • *Jacquard* Lumiere Teal Metallic paint • *Making Memories* Silver eyelet letters • *ColorBox* Cat's Eye Harbor ink • *Tsukineko* Brilliance Black ink • *Krylon* Silver leafing pen • Vellum tape • Adhesive

INSTRUCTIONS:
Background: Cut two 5" x 12" pieces of Seashell paper. Glue to bottom of Dark Blue cardstock. • **Mats**: Double-mat photos with Tan and Light Blue cardstock. Glue bottom edge of matted photos just under Seashell paper. • **Border**: With a wet paintbrush, draw 2 wavy lines on Tan mulberry paper. Tear along the lines. Glue to the top of the Seashell paper. • Tear vellum in several wavy strips. Affix to page with vellum tape. • Apply Diamond Glaze in wavy lines on the edges of the mulberry paper. Sprinkle glass beads. Let dry. • Set ¼" eyelets on each side of the vellum strip on both pages. Thread fibers through eyelets. Tape fibers to the back of the page. • **Title**: Chalk tags with Blue. Thread teal fibers through tag holes and affix "beach" stickers. Spread a thin layer of Diamond Glaze over each tag. Let dry. • Set Silver eyelets on first page. Make the apostrophe with a Silver leafing pen. Tie tags to fibers on second page. Glue in place. • **Mounts**: Cut mounts apart at hinge. Apply 2 coats of Teal Metallic paint. Let dry. Stamp swirl with Black ink. • Set ⅛" eyelets in 1 corner of each mount. Glue a faux wax seal on each mount. • Thread Tan fibers through through eyelets in mounts. Tie to Teal fibers. Glue mounts in place. • **Journaling**: Print on vellum. Sonyanna font was used in the sample. Tear to size and affix with vellum tape.

Double your joy when you share artfully arranged pages with family and friends. Try making two pages at a time... one to keep and one to share.

Sailboat Card
by Diana McMillan

Let your good wishes sail away with this wonderful sailboat card. It's sure to bring fresh sea breezes to any occasion.

MATERIALS:

Design Originals: Collage paper (#0590 Seashells); Transparency sheet (#0620 Seaside); Window Card (#0993 Large window) • Tan cardstock • *Craf-T* Decorating Chalk • Coastal Netting • Sand dollar and starfish • *JudiKins* Diamond Glaze • Fine grit sandpaper • Mounting Squares

INSTRUCTIONS:

Card: Chalk card with Brown and Tan. • Cut transparency larger than window opening. Adhere transparency window of card. • **Finish**: Tear Seashells and Tan papers as in photo. Sand papers to distress. Chalk the edges. Roll edges. Add netting, sand dollar and starfish with Diamond Glaze.

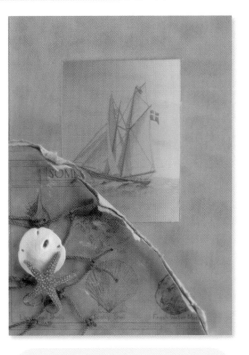

Notice the perspective in the sailboat card. Items close to you are large, while the distant sailboat is small and less distinct.

Galveston
by Amy Hubbard

Tearing paper on an angle adds variety to your scrapbook pages.

MATERIALS:

Design Originals: Collage papers (#0589 At the Beach, #0590 Seashells); Transparency sheets (#0562 Nature, #0625 Memories) • Cardstock (Ecru, Brown) • Ecru burlap 2½" x 12" • 2 Blue ⅛" eyelets • 1 Manila tag • 1 Silver mini brad • Fibers • 5 small seashells • *Marvy* Postage Stamp punch • ¹⁄₁₆" hole punch • *1001 Free Fonts* Treasure Map Deadhand • *Craft-T* Decorating Chalk - Ecru • ¾" Safety pins • Eyelet tools • *JudiKins* Diamond Glaze • Adhesive • Glue Dots

INSTRUCTIONS:

Background: Tear At the Beach paper and glue to upper corner of Brown cardstock. • Cut small holes in burlap for seashells. Adhere burlap and sea shells to the bottom of the page with Diamond Glaze. • **Mat**: Double-mat photo with Ecru cardstock and Seashells paper. Glue to page. • **Tag**: Tear a piece of Seashell paper and glue to the bottom corner of the tag. Add journaling. Attach transparency with brad. Add fibers. Adhere to page with Glue Dots. • **Title**: Attach fibers to the back of the page at the top. • Computer print title. Cut out letters with punch. Chalk letters. Punch ¹⁄₁₆" holes in the top. Pin letters to fibers.

By the Beautiful Sea
by Delores Frantz

Attractive collage needs unity. This page is a good example because the colors, papers, inks, images, mats, mounts and charms are all related to the ocean theme.

Multiple layers give depth. Torn edges add texture. Balance is achieved by using a repeated rectangle shape.

MATERIALS:
Design Originals: Collage papers (#0589 At the Beach, #0590 Seashells); Printed Mounts (#0981 Diamonds); Transparency sheet (#0620 Seaside) • Cardstock (Aqua, Turquoise, White) • *2 Creative Beginnings* Anchor charms • Cork paper • *ColorBox* Cat's Eye Aquamarine ink • Red Liner tape • Adhesive • *JudiKins* Diamond Glaze

INSTRUCTIONS:
Background: Tear Turquoise strips 3½" x 12" and 6" x 12". Tear Aqua strips 3¼" x 12" and 5¾" x 12". Tear Seashell paper strips 3" x 12" and 5½" x 12". • Ink torn edges. Layer and adhere to page according to photo. • Adhere mounts to page. • **Mat photo** with torn cork paper. Add anchor charms with E6000. • **Mounts:** Cut mount apart at hinge. Cut out transparency images. Adhere transparencies in mounts and back with White cardstock. Adhere photos in mounts. Adhere to page.

Sydney, Australia
by Kim Ivy
MATERIALS:
Design Originals: Collage paper (#0589 At the Beach); Printed Mounts (#0982 Game Pieces); Transparency sheet (#0620 Seaside) • Cardstock (Blue, Light Blue) • *Adornaments* fibers • 2 Silver jump rings • Silver eyelets (Six ⅛", thirteen ¼") • 2 Silver charms • Sand • Seahorse • Seashells • Eyelet tools • *JudiKins* Diamond Glaze • Foam Squares • Adhesive

INSTRUCTIONS:
Background: Spread Diamond Glaze evenly over the lower corner of the At the Beach paper. Dip corner into sand. Tap to remove excess. Adhere shells and seahorse with Diamond Glaze. • **Mat:** Cut Blue and Light Blue mats. Adhere mats together. Set ⅛" eyelets in Blue mat. Adhere photo with foam squares. Add jump ring to charm. Lace fibers through eyelets, adding charm. Secure fiber ends to the back of the mat. Adhere mat to page with foam squares. • **Mounts:** Set ¼" eyelets in mounts as shown in photo. Ahere photos and transparency to the back of the mounts. Weave fibers through eyelets. Adhere mounts to page with foam squares. Tie fiber ends in a bow. • **Title:** Print title on Light Blue cardstock. Cut to fit small mount. Adhere to the back of the mount. • Add jump ring to charm. Attach jump ring to title eyelet. Adhere title to page with foam squares.

You can almost smell the surf when you look at this seaside page. Waves of torn layers wash up on a beach with coastal netting, drawing attention to your family photos.

Hannah and Hunter
by Diana McMillan

This romantic page displays colors and elements that feel like the ocean.

Multiple layers give depth. Torn edges and netting add texture.

MATERIALS:
Design Originals: Collage papers (#0589 At the Beach, #0590 Seashells); Transparency sheet (#0620 Seaside) • Cardstock (Blue, Tan) • Vellum • Locket • 5 *Boxer* mini Brass brads • Coastal Netting • Sand dollar and seahorse • *JudiKins* Diamond Glaze • Mounting Squares

INSTRUCTIONS:
Background: Tear Seashells, At the Beach, and Tan papers as in photo. Roll edges. Add netting to bottom corner with Diamond Glaze. Adhere torn papers to page. • **Mat** photos with Blue cardstock. Glue to page. • **Finish**: Computer print journaling on Vellum. Tear around words. Add to page with brads. • Cut out transparency. Add to page with brads. • Place transparency, seahorse, and sand dollar inside locket. Adhere to page with Diamond Glaze.

Attach a Charm with a Jump Ring

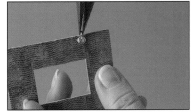

1. Thread a jump ring through the eyelet on a mount to attach a charm.

2. Close the jump ring with pliers. A twisting motion is best.

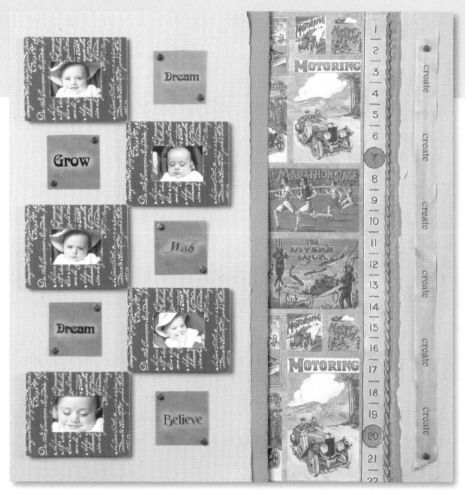

Expressions of RJ
by Diana McMillan

Small pictures repeated in a pattern make a unique layout.

MATERIALS:

Design Originals: Collage paper (#0606 Sea, Sky & Shore); Printed Mount (#0985 Dictionary); Transparency sheet (#0624 Art Words) • *Bazzill* cardstock (Pear, Leapfrog) • 12 *Boxer* mini brads • *Making Memories* word ribbon • Whale of a Punch rectangle • Mounting Squares • Zots 3-D

INSTRUCTIONS:

Background: Cut a strip of Sea, Sky & Shore paper 4" x 12". Glue to Pear cardstock. • **Right Border**: Tear a strip of Leapfrog 1⅝" x 12". Tear a strip of Pear 1⅜" x 12". Adhere strips together. Adhere ribbon with brads. Attach strip to page with Zots 3-D. • **Left Border:** Tear Leapfrog cardstock 7" x 12". Tear Pear cardstock 6½" x 12". Layer and adhere together. • Punch out transparency words. Attach to page with brads. • **Mounts**: Adhere photos to the back of the mounts. Adhere to page with Zots 3-D.

Marineland
by Amy Hubbard

This is a good example of effective layering that does not make the page thick and bulky. Notice the eyes on the fish.

There are five layers on this project. Can you find all of them?

MATERIALS:

Design Originals: Collage papers (#0605 Deep Sea, #0606 Sea, Sky & Shore); Printed Mount (#0980 Water Marks) • Blue cardstock • *Creative Imaginations* Bottle cap stickers • Black mesh • Google eyes • Fine grit sandpaper • Adhesive

INSTRUCTIONS:

Mount: Cut image from Sea, Sky & Shore paper and adhere inside mount. • **Mat**: Mat photos with Deep Sea paper. • **Finish**: Tear Deep Sea paper and adhere to cardstock. Glue eyes to fish. • Position netting and photos. Glue in place. • Glue mount to page. • Add stickers to spell title. Distress stickers with sandpaper.

Gone Fishing
by Diana McMillan

Repeating an image adds strength to the design of your scrapbook page. Cut out parts of the paper on this page and adhere with foam squares for added dimension.

MATERIALS:

Design Originals: Collage papers (2 of #0605 Deep Sea, #0493 Brown Linen); • *Bazzill* cardstock (Aloe Vera, Pear) • *Dayco* Bitty Letters die-cut • *Boxer* mini brads • Coastal netting • *JudiKins* Diamond Glaze • Zots 3-D • Mounting Squares

INSTRUCTIONS:

Background: Adhere netting from corner to corner on page with Diamond Glaze. • **Mats**: Mat photo with cardstock. Position and adhere photos with Zots 3-D. • **Title**: Attach journal box with brads. • Adhere letters in place. • **Finish**: Cut out fish and ruler from Deep Sea paper. Adhere with Zots 3-D.

The Fish Are Jumpin'
by Mary Kaye Seckler

MATERIALS:

Design Originals: Collage paper (#0605 Deep Sea); Mounts (#0989 Small Black) • Cardstock (Black, Dark Green, Olive) • 8" string • 2 small Brass ⅛" eyelets • 3 Brass fish swivel hooks • 4 fish charms • 7 Brass jump rings • 1 twig • *Collage Keepsakes* Silver stencil letters "the" • *US Stamp and Sign* ½" stencil "FISH" • *Krylon* Gold leafing pen • *Tsukineko* Opalite pigment ink (Cypress Frost, Glacier Blue, Golden Mist, Arctic Emerald), Walnut ink spray • *Adirondack* Bottle Green pad • *A Stamp In The Hand* alphabet stamps • *Hewlett Packard* transparency sheet for copiers • Hole punch (¹⁄₁₆" and ⅛") • *Scratch Art Inc* 3D-Os • Adhesive • *3M* double-stick mounting tape

INSTRUCTIONS:

Background: Tear a piece of Olive cardstock. Edge with Bottle Green ink. Stamp "are jumpin'" in Bottle Green ink. Adhere to the bottom of the page with mounting tape. • **Mat**: Tear a mat from Black cardstock. Apply Cypress Frost ink with direct-to-paper technique. Edge with Golden Mist ink. Adhere photo with mounting tape. Adhere mat to page with mounting tape. • **Title**: Paint "THE" letters with a Gold leafing pen. Adhere to Dark Green cardstock edged in leafing pen. Punch a hole in the bottom right-hand corner. Attach swivel hook with jump ring. • **Journaling**: Copy journal onto transparency. Punch an ⅛" hole in the top and bottom center and set Brass eyelets. Attach the swivel hook from the title to the transparency with a jump ring. Add swivel hook to bottom eyelet and add 3 fish charms to hook. Adhere largest fish charm with mounting tape. • Attach "THE" title piece to page with double stick mounting tape. • **Mounts**: Apply Opalite inks to Black slide mounts with direct to paper technique. Heat set. Spray Walnut ink on "FISH" stencil letters. Allow to dry. Back with Black cardstock. Insert into mounts. Punch ¹⁄₁₆" holes and attach jump rings. Attach to page with 3D-Os. • **Finish**: Slide twig through jump rings. Tie string onto twig. Add swivel hook with fish charm to the end of the string.

Looking for a different kind of journaling box? Printing on a clear transparency sheet allows the fish to show through like the view from an aquarium. Transparency sheets from Hewlett Packard are acid free.

Reflections of a Journey
by Diana McMillan

Make a daring adventure into collage with this simple layout. It only has 10 pieces on each page, so it's a good beginner project.

MATERIALS:

Design Originals: Collage papers (#0591 US Map, 2 of #0594 World Maps, #0487 Rust Linen, #0493 Brown Linen); Printed Mounts (#0981 Diamonds); Transparency sheet (#0624 Art Words); The Ephemera Book (#5207 p. 38) • Scrap of Manila cardstock • Vellum • *7gypsies* (Walnut ink, wire, paper clip, word ribbon) • *Boxer* mini brad • *Li'l Davis* Word sticker • *ColorBox* Cat's Eye Burnt Sienna ink • *AMACO WireForm* mesh • *Dritz* suspender clip • *PSX* compass stamp • *Renaissance Art* Art Keepers glass charm • *JudiKins* Diamond Glaze • *3M* Vellum tape • Mounting Squares • Zots 3-D

1. Fold the map back.

2. Flip, fold it forward.

3. Fold the corners.

4. Fold map diagonally.

5. Fold diagonal back.

6. Age edges with ink.

INSTRUCTIONS:

Background: Apply Walnut ink to World Map papers with a brush or small sponge.

REFLECTIONS OF A JOURNEY PAGE:

Title: Print words on Vellum. Tear around words. Mat Vellum on Brown Linen. • **Mat:** Mat photo with Rust Linen paper. • **Mount:** Adhere transparency words to the back of the mount. Add sticker to corner. • **Finish:** Cut out US Map. Ink edges with Burnt Sienna. Fold US Map and adhere to page with Zots 3-D. • Add large paper clip to title and photo and adhere to page with mounting squares.

BELIEVE PAGE:

Background: Adhere WireMesh with Diamond Glaze. • **Journal Box:** Journal on telegram, ink the edges. Cut out Rust Linen mat to fit Telegram. Adhere to Rust Linen with Pop Dots. Add paper clip. Adhere to page with Pop Dots. • **Mount:** Tape transparency words to the back of the mount. Ink Believe ribbon. Attach ribbon to suspender clip with brad. Attach suspender clip to mount. Adhere mount with Pop Dots. Attach ribbon to page with mounting squares. • **Finish:** Add photo with Pop Dots. • Stamp compass on scrap cardstock with Burnt Sienna ink. Assemble glass charm. • Ink "Journey" ribbon. Thread ribbon through glass charm. Adhere to page with Diamond Glaze.

Travels give us unique experiences and wonderful memories. Here's an idea for a different journal box. This one is a blank Western Union telegram from The Ephemera Book.

Travel

You can make a new map look well traveled when you age it with Walnut ink. Create that popular nostalgic look by softening the color in any background paper using this great medium. Since you control the mixing, you can get the shade you desire.

1. Mix ink crystals half-and-half with water. Drip Walnut ink onto the page. NOTE: Don't get the page too wet.

2. Spread ink over the paper with a soft brush or a small foam sponge. Let dry.

Modern Day Cowgirl
by Kim Ivy

Add a bit of western mystique to your scrapbook with conchos, brads and an old map of the West.

MATERIALS:
Design Originals: Collage papers (#0591 US Map, #0484 Blue Linen, #0487 Rust Linen); Printed Mount (#0984 Vintage Script) • *ScrapWorks* concho nailheads • 1 Brass brad • *Nostalgiques* Letter stickers • 3" of ½" wide Ecru twill • Adhesive • Zots 3-D
INSTRUCTIONS:
Background: Tear Rust Linen paper corners. Adhere with Zots 3-D. • **Mat**: Cut a Rust Linen mat ¼" larger than the photo. Glue photo to mat. • Cut a larger Blue Linen mat. Adhere photo to Blue mat. Add stickers below photo. Add nailheads. • Adhere to page with Zots 3-D. • **Mount**: Cut Blue Linen to fit mount. Print title on acetate. Layer acetate and Blue Linen. Adhere into mount. Secure ribbon to the back of the mount. Adhere mount to page. Add a brad.

1. Set the eyelets in the cardstock.

2. Lace ribbon thru the eyelets.

3. Pin ribbon to the page.

Beauty

by Kim Ivy

Although scrapbookers are encouraged to journal more, this one word says it all. This page has simple "Beauty" and a sentimental saying in the mount.

MATERIALS:

Design Originals: Collage paper (#0592 World Stamps, #0487 Rust Linen); Printed Mount (#0982 Game Pieces); Transparency sheet (#0556 Word Tags) • *Adornaments* fibers • 6 Brown eyelets • 2 pearl head pins • Game pieces • Foam tape • Adhesive

INSTRUCTIONS:

Background: Tear Rust Linen paper. Position torn pieces in opposite corners. • Position and glue photo in place. • Mark and set eyelets. Glue Rust paper in place, leaving torn edge free. Thread ribbon through eyelets. Pin ends of ribbon to secure. • **Mount**: Wrap mount with ribbon. Place foam tape on the back of the mount. Adhere transparency sheet. Glue in place. • **Title**: Glue wood tiles to page.

Sisterhood

by Delores Frantz

Tear out the middle of a paper next time you want an interesting frame. Additional layers provide color, depth, and texture. Look at the impact created by the textured paper.

MATERIALS:

Design Originals: Collage paper (#0592 World Stamps, #0547 Dictionary, #0609 Vellum Passport); Printed Mounts (#0985 Dictionary) • Cardstock (Red, Black) • Black textured paper • 8 Gold eyelets • Eyelet setter • Eyelet tools • 4 Gold brads • 24" of 1mm Black cord • *ColorBox* Cat's Eye Chestnut Roan ink • *3M* Vellum tape • ⅛" hole punch • Adhesive

INSTRUCTIONS:

Background: Tear the center from a full sheet of Red cardstock leaving 1¾" around outside edges. Tear out the center of World Stamps paper leaving 1½" around outside edges. Age torn edges with ink. Adhere to page. • Tear a 7¼" square of vellum. Adhere vellum to center of page. • **Title**: Computer generate print on Dictionary paper. Cut to size. Mat with Black cardstock. Tear Red cardstock to fit. Set eyelets. Add Black cord and brad. Adhere in place. • **Mount**: Tape photos to the back of mounts. Set eyelets. Add Black thread and brads. Glue in place.

Draw attention to your words by framing them with mounts. Allowing emotion and sentimentality into your journaling will make your page more meaningful.

Travel

True North
by Casey Rae Foree

MATERIALS:

Design Originals: Collage paper (#0596 Maps on Script); Printed mounts (#0986 Color Game); Transparency sheet (#0556 Word Tags) • Cardstock (Gray, Blue) • *ColorBox* Cat's Eye ink (Yellow Ochre, Blue) • *Encore* Gold ink • *Arrow Creative Teaching Press* spinner • Black *Zig Millennium* pen • Texture stamp • Fine grit sandpaper • Zots 3-D • *JudiKins* Diamond Glaze

INSTRUCTIONS:

Background: Tear Blue cardstock into strips 5" x 12" and 2¾" x 12". Ink the edges with Blue. Use the Texture stamp and Gold ink to scatter some random dots over the Blue paper. Write journaling. • Tear Gray cardstock into 2 strips 1" x 12". Ink the edges with Yellow Ochre. Position strips so the Gray strips extend ½" beyond the Blue. Adhere Gray strips to the Maps on Script paper. Adhere Blue strips with Pop Dots. • **Mounts**: Scuff mounts with sandpaper. Layer large mounts over words. Adhere to page with Zots 3-D. • Adhere transparency to the back of the small mount. Adhere to page with Zots 3-D. • **Finish**: Adhere photo with Zots 3-D. Adhere spinner with Diamond Glaze.

Discover Your Joy
by Mary Kaye Seckler

MATERIALS:

Design Originals: Collage papers (#0606 Sea, Sky and Shore); Printed Mounts (#0986 Color Game, #0987 Vintage Books) • Green cardstock • *Royalwood* waxed linen thread (Blue, Orange, Black, Butterscotch, Red) • Eyelets 3 each (⅛", flowers) • *Making Memories* 'Discover Your Joy' Rub-on Words • *Chatterbox* 'joy' stickers on tags • *Golden* glazes (Seafoam Green, Hunter green) • *ColorBox* Cat's Eye Evergreen ink • ⅛" hole punch • Eyelet tools • Sponge • Adhesive • *3M* double-stick mounting tape • *Glue Dots International* Pop-Up Glue Dots

INSTRUCTIONS:

Background: With a make-up sponge, streak two shades of Green glaze onto cardstock. • Tear corners from Sea, Sky and Shore paper. Ink the edges with Evergreen. Glue to corners of painted cardstock. • **Mounts**: Cut large slide mounts in half. Snip ⅛" slit in each outside corner. Wrap each corner with waxed linen thread tucking the thread into the slit to prevent slippage and tie on back of mount. • Punch a ⅛" hole in bottom center of each mount. Set eyelet in each hole. Set matching flower eyelet in each tag hole. • Add 'joy' letters to tags. Tie each tag to matching slide mount with waxed linen thread. • Adhere photos to mounts with Pop-Up Glue Dots. Adhere mounts to page with double-stick mounting tape. • **Title**: Apply 'Discover your Joy' rub-ons to Green cardstock. Note: Piece the word 'your' together from other words on the sheet. Take the word 'joy' from 'enjoy'. • Trim the cardstock into two pieces and round the corners. Edge with Evergreen ink. Streak the same glazes over the rub-ons with a make-up sponge. Adhere to page with tape.

Give your pages a unique look when you present mounted photos on an antiqued paper canvas. It's easy to sponge two different glazes to create this artistic effect.

10 Things We Love About Betty

by Mary Kaye Seckler

This is a fantastic idea for a group project. Get the family together and have them list their favorite things about a loved one.

Then, make this page to honor that special person.

This is a great birthday gift.

MATERIALS:
Design Originals: Collage paper (#0613 Walnut Scroll, #0493 Brown Linen) • Cardstock (Black, Dark Brown) • 5 *Making Memories* Brown brads • *Offray* sheer Gold ribbon • *Adornaments* Brown fibers • Brown *Magic Mesh* • Various charms • Letter beads • Brown *Royalwood* waxed linen thread • *Sizzix (*Fun Serif Die Alphabet, Script Die Alphabet, Scallop Tag Die-cut) • *Paper Shapers* Intricate Iris Corner Adorner • *Tsukineko* Versacolor Cubes (Bark, Black) • Awl • *EK Success* glue pen • *Glue Dots International* (Glue Dots, Pop-Up Glue Dots)

INSTRUCTIONS:
Background: Tie charms onto mesh with waxed linen thread. Affix mesh to paper with Brown brads. • **Title:** Punch Intricate Iris pattern 4 times evenly spaced across the top of Walnut Scroll paper. Thread ribbon through the punch pattern. Affix to back of paper with Glue Dots. • Die-cut 10 small tags with Sizzix scallop tag die. Edge with Bark ink. Write '10 Things' on tags. Thread fibers through tag holes. Tie onto ribbon in pairs. Affix tags to paper with Glue Dots. • Punch '10 Things' in black cardstock and Brown Linen paper using Fun Serif alphabet. Adhere Black and Brown letters together in shadow style with Brown on top. • Punch 'We Love About Betty' in Black cardstock and Brown Linen paper using Script alphabet letters and shadows. Adhere letters to shadows and title letters in place. • **Mat:** Tear Dark Brown cardstock mat to size. Wet edges and curl. Edge with Black ink. Adhere photo with Glue Dots. Thread 'Betty' letter beads on Brown waxed linen thread. Punch two holes in mat using an awl. Thread linen through holes and tie on back of mat. Affix photo mat to mesh with Pop-Up Glue Dots.

10 Things We Love About Betty

10.
Your Bowling Average

9.
Your Dance Skills

8.
Your Organization

7.
Your Energy

6.
Your Imagination

5.
Your Love of Life

4.
Your Persistence

3.
Your Generosity

2.
Your Sense of Humor

1.
The Way You Love Us

1. Punch Iris pattern across the top of the page.

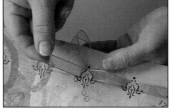

2. Thread ribbon through the holes.

3. Tie tags across the ribbon about every inch.

Walnut & Vellum

Family Memories
by Delores Frantz

Make a unique title with bottle caps and copper color leather letters.

Upholstery tacks on the mount give added texture to this layout.

MATERIALS:

Design Originals Collage papers (#0598 Game Cards, #0613 Walnut Scroll); Mounts (#0991 Large White) • Dark Brown Cardstock • *ColorBox* Cat's Eye Chestnut Roan ink • *EK Success* round Copper color letter stickers • 6 Bottle caps • 8 upholstery nails • 1" Circle punch • Wire cutters • Hammer • Pad of newspaper • Adhesive

INSTRUCTIONS:

Mat: Double-mat photo on Brown cardstock and Game Cards paper. • **Mount**: Cover mount with Game Cards paper. Glue photo in mount. • **Title**: Place bottle caps right side up on a pad of newspaper. Tap with a hammer until the edges curl upward. Punch 6 circles from Brown cardstock. Apply letter stickers to circles. Glue circles in bottle caps. Glue caps down the left side of the Scroll paper. • **Finish**: Cut 3 card images from Cards paper. Glue to page. • Cut shanks from tacks. Glue to corners of photo and mount.

This page is an excellent example of unity. The tan bricks in the background of the photo work really well with the Walnut paper. The buckle on the border could easily have been part of the costume. The orange color mounts and transparencies match the Halloween theme.

Wendy the Friendly Witch
by Delores Frantz

MATERIALS:

Design Originals: Collage papers (#0617 Music, #0608 Vellum Shorthand); Printed Mounts (#0983 Tapes); Transparency sheet (#0626 Holidays 2) • Cardstock (Black, White, Peach, Brown) • 13" Black 5/8" wide grosgrain ribbon • *Dritz* Fray Check • Nickel 7/8" buckle • *Making Memories* round alphabet charms • 10 Nickel eyelets • 1/8" Hole punch • Eyelet tools • E6000 glue • Adhesive

INSTRUCTIONS:

Background: Tear these strips: 4" x 12" Vellum Shorthand, 4¾" x 12" Brown cardstock, 5½" x 12" Black cardstock. Layer and adhere to the right side of the Music paper. • Thread buckle on ribbon. Cut one end to a point and apply Fray Check to cut edge. Center and adhere ribbon on vellum. • **Mounts**: Print date on Peach cardstock and glue in small mount. • Adhere transparencies in mounts. Back with White cardstock. Use eyelets to attach mounts to ribbon. • **Mat**: Tear Black cardstock. Mat photo and adhere to page. • **Title**: Adhere letter rounds under the photo.

Treasure Island
by Diana McMillan

MATERIALS:

Design Originals: Collage paper (#0613 Walnut Scroll, #0615 Words, #0618 Water Marks, #0608 Vellum Shorthand, #0493 Brown Linen) • *Creative Beginnings* Gold butterfly charm • *Fiber Scraps* fibers • *ColorBox* Cat's Eye Chestnut Roan ink • *JudiKins* Diamond Glaze • Vellum tape • Mounting Squares • Zots 3-D

INSTRUCTIONS:

Background: Cut Walnut Words paper 5" x 12". Ink the edges. Adhere to Vellum. • Tear Vellum paper ½" larger on top and bottom of Walnut Words paper. • Adhere to Water Marks paper with Zots 3-D. • **Mat**: Cut Brown Linen mat large enough for your photo and journaling space. Cut Walnut Scroll paper ½" larger on each side. Cut Brown Linen ¼" larger on each side. Layer photo and mats. Glue together. Record journaling. Adhere to page with Zots 3-D. • **Finish**: Crisscross several fibers. Tape fiber ends to the back of the page. Adhere butterfly charm to page with Diamond Glaze.

Create a beautiful layout in minutes with multiple layers and a combination of papers.

Play Me A Song
by Diana McMillan

Celebrate your virtuoso with themed papers, transparencies, and colors that make your pages sing!

MATERIALS:

Design Originals: Collage papers (#0617 Music, #0608 Shorthand); Printed Mounts (#0987 Vintage Books); Transparency sheet (#0558 Script) • Cardstock (Black, Red) • Vellum • 4 *Boxer* mini Black brads • 2 *Creative Beginnings* Gold music charms • *JudiKins* Diamond Glaze • Mounting Squares • Zots 3-D

INSTRUCTIONS:

Title: Print title and journaling on vellum. Cut out and attach to page with brads. • **Mounts**: Tape transparency and photos to the back of the mounts. Adhere charms to mounts with Diamond Glaze. Adhere mounts to page with Pop Dots. • **Mat**: Cut 3 edges ¼" around photo. Cut bottom edge to 1" and tear. Cut a strip of Vellum Shorthand, Red and Black cardstock 1" by the length of photo. Layer strips together and adhere to Black mat. Affix photo to mat with Zots 3-D. Adhere to page.

Dream
by Diana McMillan

Here's a new use for mounts... page corners!

1. Place Vellum over your photo. Use a ruler & pencil to draw around focal point of the photo.

2. Cut window in vellum with a ruler & craft knife.

3. Ink the edges of the window.

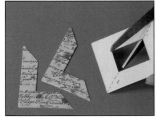

4. Adhere vellum to page with vellum tape.

MATERIALS:
Design Originals: Collage papers (#0610 Vellum Memories, #0615 Walnut Words); Printed Mounts (#0984 Vintage Script) • *Blue Moon Beads* word tag • 1 jump ring • *Making Memories* word ribbon • *ColorBox* Cat's Eye Chestnut Roan ink • Craft knife • Cutting mat • Vellum tape • Zots 3-D
INSTRUCTIONS:
Background: Glue photo to Walnut paper • **Vellum**: Place Vellum over page. Mark position for windows. Use a cutting mat and craft knife to cut windows. Ink the window edges. Adhere to Walnut paper. • **Finish**: Attach jump ring to word bead and tag. String ribbon through jump ring. Wrap ribbon around page and secure ends to the back. • Cut mounts at an angle to make corner pieces. Adhere corners to page.

Key to My Heart
by Diana McMillan
MATERIALS:
Design Originals: Collage papers (#0595 Vintage Script, #0607 Vellum Sentiments, #0612 Vellum Keys); Printed Mount (#0985 Dictionary) • Black cardstock • 4 *Boxer* mini brads • *Making Memories* ribbon • *Offray* ribbon • Vintage key • *ColorBox* Cat's Eye Chestnut Roan ink • *7gypsies* Walnut ink • *JudiKins* Diamond Glaze • Zots 3-D
INSTRUCTIONS:
Background: Tint Vintage Script paper with Walnut ink. Let dry. Tear lower corner as shown. Ink edges with Chestnut Roan. • Tear a corner of Vellum Keys. Adhere script to Vellum Keys to fit page. •
Mount: Ink the edges with Chestnut Roan. Tape Vellum Sentiments to back of mount. Adhere to page with Zots 3-D. •
Mat: Mat photo with Black cardstock. Adhere to page with Zots 3-D. • **Title**: Computer print on Vellum Keys paper. Tear around title. Ink edges with Chestnut Roan. Attach with brads. • **Finish**: Adhere key with Diamond Glaze. Secure ribbon to back of page.

Cherish tender moments with delicate Vellum papers and a soft script background. Pretty fonts add elegance to this page.

Vintage keys and cherished memorabilia take you back to a romantic time.

5. Cut mount at an angle to make corner pieces.

6. Glue corners to the page.

Jeanette Raffenaud
by Diana McMillan

MATERIALS:

Design Originals: Collage papers (#0607 Vellum Sentiments, #0609 Vellum Passport, #0613 Walnut Scroll); Printed mount (#0987 Vintage Books); The Ephemera Book #5207 • Cardstock (Peach, Black) • Pair of glasses • 3 Tan eyelets • *ColorBox* Cat's Eye Chestnut Roan ink • Eyelet tools • *JudiKins* Diamond Glaze • Mounting Squares • Zots 3-D • Vellum Tape

INSTRUCTIONS:

Background: Glue Vellum Passport to Peach cardstock. • Tear a triangle of Vellum Passport. Ink the edge. Adhere to page with eyelets. • **Title**: Tear "Memories" from Walnut Scroll paper. Ink the edges. Adhere to page with Zots 3-D. • **Mats**: Cut Black cardstock and Walnut Scroll to mat photo. Adhere mats together. Adhere to page with Zots 3-D. • Print name on Vellum Passport. Adhere to photo with Vellum tape. • **Mount**: Tape Vellum Sentiment to the back of the mount. Glue mount to page. • **Finish**: Cut images, receipts, and letters from pages 19, 33, 37, 39, and 41 in The Ephemera Book. Tuck into pocket. Adhere in place if preferred. • Glue glasses to pocket with Diamond Glaze.

This pocket provides a wonderful place to keep all the written memorabilia from a loved one. Make this very special remembrance for someone you love.

Twins
by Delores Frantz

Layers give dimension to this attractive page. The first layers are torn papers. The next contains mats and mounts. Gold cord and charming angels provide a sparkling finish.

MATERIALS:

Design Originals: Collage papers (#0609 Vellum Passport, #0610 Vellum Memories, #0612 Vellum Keys, #0549 Shorthand); Printed Mounts (#0980 Water Marks); Transparency sheet (#0625 Memories) • Cardstock (Light Gold, Turquoise) • *ColorBox* Cat's Eye Yellow Ochre ink • 4 Gold eyelets • 3 *Jesse James* 1" angels • 36" of Gold 1 mm cord • 1/8" hole punch • Eyelet tools • Adhesive • *JudiKins* Diamond Glaze

INSTRUCTIONS:

Background: Tear a 2½" strip of each Vellum and three 3" strips of Gold cardstock. Apply ink to edges. • Adhere a Vellum strip to each Gold paper strip. Adhere to Shorthand paper. • **Mat** photo on Turquoise cardstock. Set eyelets in corners. Thread braid through eyelets. Secure ends on back of mat. • **Mounts**: Adhere transparencies in mounts and angels to mounts. Adhere to page.

Time Flies
by Diana McMillan

MATERIALS:

Design Originals: Collage papers (#0611 Vellum Clocks, #0618 Water Marks); Printed mounts (#0984 Vintage Script); Transparency sheet (#0560 Objects) • *Bazzill* cardstock (Apricot, Yam) • *DMD* Clock face • 2 spinner hands • 1 Gold eyelet • *Craf-T* Decorating Chalks • Eyelet tools • *JudiKins* Diamond Glaze • Mounting Squares • Zots 3-D

INSTRUCTIONS:

Background: Adhere Vellum to Water Marks paper. • **Border**: Cut Apricot cardstock 2⅜" x 12". Cut Yam cardstock 2" x 12". Layer and adhere to page. • **Mounts**: Adhere photos and transparency to the back of the mounts. Adhere to page with Zots 3-D. • **Clock**: Chalk clock face. Attach clock hands together with eyelet. Glue to clock with Diamond Glaze. • **Clock**: Glue clock to mount. Adhere mount to page with Zots 3-D.

What a great way to display a series of "growing up" photos. This would also make a wonderful presentation at a 50th anniversary using pictures that cover a couple's married life.

Make sure you include some everyday shots along with the "momentous holiday" photos. It will make your page composition much more interesting.

1. Chalk the clock face with a tan color.

2. Attach 2 clock hands together with an eyelet.

3. Adhere clock hands with Diamond Glaze.

Celebrate the holidays all year long. Holidays with family and children are one of our most precious memories.

Trick or Treat

by Stephanie Greenwood

MATERIALS:

Design Originals: Collage papers (#0574 Pumpkins, #0575 Trick or Treat, #0493 Brown Linen); Printed Mount (#0983 Tapes); Transparency sheet (#0626 Holidays 2) • *ColorBox* Cat's Eye ink (Green, Chestnut Roan) • Foam Squares

INSTRUCTIONS:

Mat: Cut Brown Linen ½" larger than the photo. Adhere photo to mat with foam squares. • Tear Trick or Treat paper with an inch border around the matted photo. Ink the edges. Adhere matted photo to torn mat with foam squares. Adhere to page. • **Mount**: Ink the edges with Chestnut Roan. Adhere transparencies to the back of the mount. Back the transparency with Trick or Treat paper. Adhere to page with foam squares. • **Title**: Tear "trick or treat" words from Pumpkins paper. Adhere to page with foam squares.

Tis the Season

by Delores Frantz

MATERIALS:

Design Originals: Collage papers (#0566 Music, #0567 French Horns, #0572 Green Holly); Mounts (#0989 Small Black); Transparency sheet (#0559 Alphabet) • Black cardstock • Black 24 gauge wire • 16 Gold eyelets • *Sizzix* die-cutter and alphabet dies • ⅛" circle punch • Eyelet tools

INSTRUCTIONS:

Background: Cut French Horns paper 11½" x 11½". Glue to Black cardstock. • **Title**: Die-cut letters. Glue to page. • **Mounts**: Tape transparency letters to the back of the mounts. Set eyelets in mount corners. Glue mounts to page. • **Mats**: Cut Music paper and Black mats to fit photo. Glue mats together. Set eyelets. • Curl wire sections and insert through eyelets. Tape ends to the back of the mat. Glue mat to page. • **Finish**: Cut out 5 holly clusters from Green Holly paper. Glue to mounts and page.

Halloween is so much fun and it's even more fun to scrapbook the memories and those special costumes and events. Beautiful papers provide the perfect backdrop. Multi-layer mats make your photos stand out.

Happy Halloween
by Stephanie Greenwood

MATERIALS:

Design Originals: Collage papers (#0573 Halloween Collage, #0575 Trick or Treat, #0487 Rust Linen); Printed Mounts (#0983 Tapes); Transparency sheet (#0626 Holidays 2) • *Bazzill* Pear cardstock • Green raffia • *ColorBox* Cat's Eye ink (Chestnut Roan, Green) • Mounting Squares • Foam Squares

INSTRUCTIONS:

Background: Tear Rust Linen 3½" x 12". Ink the edge with Chestnut Roan. • Tear Trick or Treat paper 3¼" x 12". Ink the edge with Green. Layer and adhere papers together. Adhere to page with foam squares. • **Mounts**: Ink the edges with Chestnut Roan. Adhere transparencies to the back of the mounts. Wrap raffia around the bottom of the large mount. Adhere to page with foam squares. • **Mats**: Cut a double mat of Pear and Rust Linen for each photo. Ink the edges with Chestnut Roan and Green. Adhere photos to mats with foam squares. Adhere to page with foam squares.

Halloween 2002
by Diana McMillan

MATERIALS:

Design Originals: Collage papers (#0576 Halloween Postcards, #0481 Teal Linen) • Printed Mount (#0984 Vintage Script) • Transparency sheet (#0626 Holidays 2) • Vellum • Scrap of Manila cardstock • 8 *Happy Hammer* Orange brads • *Nunn Design* square Copper charm • *Fiber Scraps* Monochromatic Orange fibers • *ColorBox* Cat's Eye ink (Chestnut Roan) • Mounting Squares • Foam Squares

INSTRUCTIONS:

Mat: Trace around photo on the Halloween Postcards paper. Add a ¼" all the way around. Cut out window. • Ink edges. • Adhere photo to Teal Linen with foam squares. • **Title**: Adhere transparency to bottom of Halloween paper with brads. • **Journal box**: Computer print journaling on Vellum. Adhere to Halloween paper with brads. • **Mount**: Ink the edges. Tape photo to the back of the mount. Adhere to page with foam squares. • Write age on small square of Manila cardstock. Thread fiber through charm. Wrap fiber around Halloween paper and secure in back. Secure charm to mount. • **Finish**: Adhere Halloween paper to Teal paper with foam squares.

The best thing about holidays are the memories. Enhance your holiday memories with ribbon, charms and the glisten of brass spirals.

Noel
by Delores Frantz

MATERIALS:

Design Originals: Collage papers (#0565 Christmas Collage, #0568 Angels Tapestry) • Light Green cardstock • 12" of Rust 1½" ribbon • 24 and 28 gauge Copper wire • Amber seed beads • 6 Gold ⅜" brads • 5 Gold wire spirals • 1⅜" Gold ornate charm • *Craf-T* Decorating Chalk (Brown) • Foam Squares • Adhesive

INSTRUCTIONS:

Background: Cut Angels Tapestry paper 11½" x 11½". Glue to Green cardstock. • **Title**: Thread beads on 24 gauge wire. Write "Noel" on paper to use as a pattern . Shape letters using the pattern as a guide. Attach beaded word to cardstock with 28 gauge wire. • Attach coils to title by stringing beads on 24 gauge wire, coil, then go through wire again to back of title.. Alternate with 8 beads on next spiral. Adhere to page. • **Mats**: Cut Green mat to fit photo. Adhere photo to mat. Affix spiral charms to corners and mat to page. • **Finish**: Adhere ribbon and charm in place. Tear Angel from Collage paper. Chalk edges with Brown. Adhere to page with foam squares.

Gingerbread Cookies
by Delores Frantz

MATERIALS:

Design Originals: Collage papers (#0570 Diamonds with Holly, #0571 Red Holly, #0572 Green Holly, #0478 Green Linen) • Vellum • White cardstock • 12 Red buttons • 4 Gingerbread cutouts • Gold metallic thread • *Fiskars* decorative scissors • Needle • Adhesive • Glue Dots • Foam Squares

INSTRUCTIONS:

Background: Cut Diamonds with Holly paper 11½" x 11½". Glue to Green Linen paper. • **Title**: Print title on Vellum. Cut out. Adhere to page with Glue Dots. Add heart buttons with Glue Dots. • **Mats**: Cut

Green Linen paper mats. Cut Holly paper ½" smaller than Green Linen. • Cut a hole in the center of the Holly paper. Tear and roll pieces back to make frames. Glue photo to Green Linen mat. Center rolled frame over photo. Glue in place. • Sew a Gold metallic thread around the edge of Holly paper. Tape thread ends to the back of the mat. Glue mats to page. • **Finish**: Cut pieces of White rick rack cardstock with decorative scissors. Glue to gingerbread men. Draw faces. Add buttons. Adhere to page with foam squares.

Christmas is one of the most photographed holidays of the year. Enhance your holiday pages with coordinated papers, mounts, and transparencies.

Mom, Who's Taking Our Picture?
by Delores Frantz

MATERIALS:

Design Originals: Collage papers (#0569 Santas, #0547 Dictionary) • Red cardstock • 3 Red buttons • 4 Brass upholstery nails • 40 Gold eyelets • Red ribbon • 1 Red tassel • 1 tag • Fiskars decorative edge scissors • Eyelet tools • *JudiKins* Diamond Glaze • Adhesive • Foam Squares

INSTRUCTIONS:

Background: Set eyelets around the edge of Santa paper. Lace ribbon through eyelets. Tape end to the back of the page. • **Mat**: Use decorative scissors to cut Red mat for photo. Adhere photo to Red mat. Cut Dictionary paper ½" larger than Red mat. Adhere Red mat to Dictionary paper, then to the center of the page. • Cut off the head from the upholstery nails. Glue to page with Diamond Glaze. • **Tag**: Cover tag with Dictionary paper. Write "Christmas 2001" on the tag. Attach tassel. Adhere to page with foam squares. • **Finish**: Cut holly leaves from Santa paper. Adhere to Red cardstock. Cut out. • Glue buttons to leaves. Adhere to page with foam squares.

Bright decorative papers preserve special Holiday memories.

Wrap It Up
by Delores Frantz
photo on page 44

MATERIALS:

Design Originals: Collage paper (#0571 Red Holly, #0572 Green Holly, #0478 Green Linen) • Printed Mount (#0988 Small White, #0991 Large White) • Transparency sheet (#0563 Holidays) • 6 Silver stars • *DMC* Burgundy Pearl Cotton • Game Piece letters Adhesive • *JudiKins* Diamond Glaze • Foam Squares

INSTRUCTIONS:

Background: Trim Green Linen paper to 11" x 11". • Thread pearl cotton through stars. Cut pearl cotton to desired length. Tape to Green Linen paper so the ends will be under the photo mat and under the Green Holly strips. Tape the ends of 2 star threads to the back of the page at the top. • Cut 4 strips of Green Holly 1" x 11". Glue to Green Linen paper. Adhere Green Linen paper to Red Holly paper. • **Mat**: Cut Red Holly paper mat for photo, adhere photo to mat and mat to page. • **Mounts**: Cover mounts with Holly paper. Insert photo and transparency. Adhere Red mount to page. Adhere small mount with foam squares. Tie 2 bows of pearl cotton. Adhere on top of mounts. • **Title**: Glue game piece letters to page with Diamond Glaze.

Santa and Me
by Diana McMillan

MATERIALS:

Design Originals: Collage papers (#0569 Santas, #0570 Diamonds with Holly, #0572 Green Holly, #0489 Rust Floral); Printed Mount (#0987 Vintage Books); Transparency sheet (#0626 Holidays 2) • Gold Santa charm • 2 beads • Gold hoop • 1 Red eyelet • *ColorBox* Cat's Eye ink (Scarlet, Green, Chestnut Roan) • *Carolee's Creations* Red glue glitter pen • Eyelet tools • Mounting Squares • Zots 3-D

INSTRUCTIONS:

Background: Tear Diamonds with Holly at an angle to fit the lower corner of the page. Ink the edge. Apply glue glitter to berries. Let dry. Attach to Santas paper with Zots 3-D. • **Mat**: Cut Green Holly paper to fit photo. Ink edges with Green. • Tear 2 pieces of Brown Linen paper 1" larger than Green Holly mat. Adhere torn pirces back to back and ink edges with Chestnut Roan. Curl edges with your fingers. • Set eyelet in the lower corner of the photo. Assemble charms, beads, and tags on hoop. Attach to eyelet. • Adhere mat layers with Zots 3-D. • **Mount**: Adhere transparency to the back of the mount. Adhere to page with Zots 3-D.

Games with Grandma
by Donna Kinsey

Collage is an excellent medium to express accumulated memories. This page recalls all the different games we played at Grandma's house. Journal tags record special moments.

MATERIALS:
Design Originals: Collage paper (#0579 ABCs Dictionary, #0598 Game Cards, #0603 Checkerboard, #0604 Target) • Cardstock (Red, Black, White) • Game Pieces • *Li'l Davis* Epoxy Red w Black bubble letters • *Provo Craft* Alphabitties • *Westrim* Mosaic Magic letter tiles, silver charms • *Sizzix* 3 tag die cuts • Metallic Rouge thread • *DMC* floss (Red, Black) • *Adornaments* fibers (Red, Black, White) • 14 Red eyelets • *Hoyle* playing cards • Washer • Bottle caps • Metal spacer beads • 8" x 8" Black tulle • Buttons (Black, Red) • *ColorBox* Cat's Eye ink (Red, Black) • Eyelet tools • ¼" hole punch • Large eye needle • Sponge • Pop Dots • Red Liner tape • Glue stick

GAMES WITH GRANDMA PAGE:
INSTRUCTIONS:
Background: Sponge the edges of Red cardstock with Black ink. • **Tags**: Cut 1 large Red, 1 large White, 1 medium Black, 1 medium White. Name your favorite card game using Alphabitties letters on a White medium tag. Layer it on a Red tag. • Cut out 2 cards from the Game Cards paper. Glue to a medium Black tag and a large White tag. • Layer the large Red and White tags. Tie together with fibers. • **Card fan**: Tear a fan from Black cardstock. Punch a hole at the point and thread fibers. Adhere fan to page. • Mat photo and adhere it to the fan with Pop Dots. • Cut out cards from Game Cards paper. • Position the cards around the photo and adhere to page. • **Bottom pocket**: Tear a Black piece of cardstock 4½" x 11". Tear a White piece of cardstock 3½" x 10". Sponge with Red ink. • Glue White to Black. • Tear a playing card in half. Glue to each side of the White paper. • Cut 2 pieces of tulle. Use eyelets, buttons, and washers to adhere tulle. Attach letters and domino. Wrap fibers around sides and top of pocket. • **Finish**: Position pocket on bottom of Red cardstock. Attach by setting eyelets. Thread 4 strands of metallic Red and 6 strands of Black floss. Sew threads through eyelets and around paper with your favorite stitch. • Use Red Liner tape to adhere tags, bottle caps, and poker chips. • Sew metal bead and small Black button to Black tag.

TIC TAC TOE PAGE:
INSTRUCTIONS:
Background: Sponge the edges of Red cardstock with Black ink. • Collage papers at random onto Red cardstock. • **Tags**: Cut 2 large Red, 1 large Black, 1 large White, 2 medium White, 2 medium Red, 1 small White. • Layer a medium Red tag onto a large Black. Layer a medium White on a large Red. • Journal on desired tags. • Add fibers. • Attach to collage with Pop Dots, eyelets, or buttons. • **Finish**: Add game pieces, tulle, bottle cap, Checkerboard, and letters. • Add buttons with beads to tic-tac-toe boards with Red and Black floss.

Hunter Plays Pool
by Stephanie Greenwood

Action shots are much more interesting than posed photos, so take lots of pictures of your children doing fun things - exploring, playing, learning. You will be happier with your scrapbook pages when they include an activity.

MATERIALS:

Design Originals: Collage paper (#0604 Target); Printed Mounts (#0985 Dictionary); Transparency sheet (#0623 Games) • Red cardstock • Vellum • 1 Red brad • 2 Spinner arrows • *Walnut Hollow* clock face • Adhesive • *JudiKins* Diamond Glaze • Mounting Squares • Foam Squares • Vellum Tape

INSTRUCTIONS:

Background: Adhere clock face to the center of the target with Diamond Glaze. • Hold spinners together with a brad. Adhere spinners to page with foam squares. • **Mounts**: Print journaling on Vellum. Cut to fit mount. • Tape transparency, photos, and Vellum to the back of the mounts. Cut Red cardstock mat ½" larger than the mount. Adhere mat to mount with foam squares. **Finish:** Adhere mounts to page.

It's Your Move
by Stephanie Greenwood

MATERIALS:

Design Originals: Collage papers (#0601 Old Game Pieces, #0603 Checkerboard); Mounts (#0989 Small Black); Transparency sheet (#0623 Games) • Cardstock (Red, Black) • Game Pieces • 9 pocket slide mount holder • Foam Squares • Mounting squares • Vellum Tape • *JudiKins* Diamond Glaze

INSTRUCTIONS:

Background: Adhere pockets to Checkerboard with Vellum tape. • **Mounts**: Cover 2 mounts with Old Game Pieces paper. Tape transparencies to the back of mounts. Insert mounts in pockets. • **Mat**: Double-mat photo with Black and Red. Attach to page with foam squares. • **Finish**: Adhere checkers to page with Diamond Glaze.

This page is really fun... open the Bingo card to reveal more photos!

The Games People Play
by Mary Kaye Seckler

Collage is appealing because it gives the viewer a lot to interact with. This layout offers 2 hinged doors with more surprises inside. The different sized pieces and changing textures keep your eye moving on the page. The colors are just as bright and happy as the subjects in the photos.

Don't be intimidated by these collage pages. Just put them together, Layer by Layer Scrapbooks.

MATERIALS:
Design Originals: Collage papers (#0601 Old Game Pieces, #0616 Walnut Water Spots); Printed Mounts (#0980 Water Marks, #0989 Small Black); Transparency sheet (#0623 Games) • The Ephemera Book (#5207 p. 17, 19) • Manila cardstock for transparency mat • Scraps of colored cardstock for "People" letters • 4 *Making Memories* Silver hinges • Sticker Studio "Oh" letters • *Jolee's* Scrabble Accents • *Accu-Cut* (Tag dies, "People" letters) • 1 chess charm • 2 Brass brads • 1 Brass fishing swivel • 7 assorted color 1/8" eyelets • 1 Red 1/4" eyelet • Game pieces• 1 Library card and envelope • *ColorBox* Cat's Eye ink (Chestnut, Scarlet, Turquoise, Merlot, Violet, Midnight) • *Adirondack* Caramel ink • Stipple brush • *Stamp Camp* game stamps • Metal ruler • *PVA* glue • *Hermafix* adhesive

INSTRUCTIONS:

Background: Tear 4 strips of Red cardstock 3/4" x 12" using a ruler. Age with Chestnut ink. Glue 2 strips to each page as in photo.

Titles: Cut tags from Walnut Water Spots paper. Adhere stickers for "OH". Add brads and eyelets. Glue tag to page. • Glue tag and game pieces for "THE" in place. • Cut "People" letter tags from Walnut Water Spots paper. Cut out the same tags again from colored cardstock. Attach "People" tags to page with eyelets. • Cut mounts apart at hinge. Layer acetate and manila behind mount. Attach with Hermafix. Punch a 1/8" hole in the lower right corner of the Games mount. Attach fishing swivel and chess charm. Attach to title with PVA glue.

...continued on page 49

Check out this fun surprise... open the game card to reveal photos and an envelope!

The Games People Play, continued from page 48...

Mats: Tear cardstock and edge with matching ink to make mats for game boards and photos. Attach to page with Hermafix.

Eyelet Hinges: Mat image from The Ephemera Book on Purple cardstock. Age edges with ink. Stipple library card and envelope with Caramel ink. Stamp "Scores and Highlights". Glue library pocket to the back. Record game scores on library card. Insert into envelope. Glue a strip of cardstock to the back of the Games paper to support the hinges. Punch holes and set eyelet hinges. Glue game pieces with PVA. • Mat Bingo card from Ephemera book on Red cardstock. Attach spinner with eyelet. Adhere matted photos to the back of the card. Reinforce the back of the Game Pieces paper in the hinge area with a piece of cardstock. Punch holes and set hinges. Adhere photo to page under Bingo card.

Games We Play
by Kim Ivy

People have always played games. Make a page that recalls the fun of your family game night. Use old game pieces to embellish your page, and if you have been saving those old score cards, you can put them to good use here.

MATERIALS:

Design Originals: Collage papers (#0602 Game Pieces, #0616 Spots, #0618 Water Marks, #0481 Teal Linen); Printed Mounts (#0986 Color Game); Transparency sheet (#0623 Games) • Li'l Davis circle letters • Foam Squares • Adhesive • Corner rounder

INSTRUCTIONS:

Background: Tear a strip of Teal paper 3" x 12". Tear Water Marks paper 2½" x 12". Tear Game Pieces paper 2" x 12". Layer strips along the left side of Spots paper and adhere together. Adhere to page with Pop Dots. • **Mats:** Cut mats from Teal paper, round corners. Cut a frame from Game Pieces paper for the large photo, round corners. Tape photo to frame. Glue framed photo to mat. • **Mounts:** Adhere transparencies to the back of the mount. Cover the back of the transparency with Walnut Ink paper and tape it to the back of the mount. Adhere mount to Teal mat with foam squares. Glue to page. • **Finish:** Glue circle letters to page.

Fun and Games
by Delores Frantz

This collage is appealing because it has balance and good color coordination. The domino papers above the photo offset the heavier tiles below.

MATERIALS:
Design Originals: Collage paper (#0598 Game Cards, #0600 Dominoes) • Black cardstock • Red handmade paper • *ColorBox* Cat's Eye Chestnut Roan Ink • 5 star ⅞" brads • Maroon letter tiles • Adhesive • *JudiKins* Diamond Glaze

INSTRUCTIONS:
Background: Cut images from Dominoes paper. Ink the edges. Position and glue to page. • **Mat:** Double mat photo with Black cardstock and torn Red paper. Glue to page. • **Title:** Adhere game pieces with Diamond Glaze. • **Finish:** Adhere stars to page with Diamond Glaze.

Grow
by Diana McMillan

Connect your page to an event by completing journal tags. Your page will tell a story your children will want to hear.

MATERIALS:
Design Originals: Collage papers (#0601 Old Game Pieces, #0493 Brown Linen); Printed Mounts (#0982 Game Pieces); Transparency sheet (#0624 Art Words) • Black cardstock • *Adornaments* fibers • 1 Red brad • Tags (1 Manila, 1 Black) • Mounting Squares • Zots 3-D

INSTRUCTIONS:
Background: Tear 2 strips of Black cardstock 1½" x 12". Adhere to top and bottom of page. • Tear Old Game Pieces paper slightly smaller than Black cardstock. Adhere with Zots 3-D. • **Large Mounts:** Adhere photos to the back of the mounts. Tear Black cardstock to mat 2 mounts. Adhere cardstock and mounts with Zots 3-D. • **Tags:** Journal on the manila tag. Attach Black and Manila tags together with Red brad. Add fibers to brad. Adhere tags to page with Zots 3-D. • **Small Mount:** Cut out transparency and tape to the back of the small mount. • Adhere small mount to tag with Zots 3-D. • **Finish:** Add photo to bottom corner with Zots 3-D.

Mary Kaye Seckler
creates wonderful paper arts.

Lisa Vollrath
loves to work with papers of all kinds.

Kim Ivy
teaches classes for scrapbooks and paper arts.

Donna Kinsey
loves to learn something new every day.

Stephanie Greenwood
is an established art teacher and avid scrapbooker.

Casey Rae Foree
scrapbooks and works with creative papers.